# Ten Modern Quilts

Basil Papanastassiou

I0212381

Copyright 2015 Basil Papanastassiou

Published by BasilQuilts!, Burt & Basil Publishing, a division of The Two Session Solution, Inc.

Photography by Woodbury & Associates Photography, Pompano Beach, Florida (http://www.wa-digital.com).

All rights reserved. No part of this book may be reproduced in any form without the express permission of the author. The patterns contained herein are for the personal use of the purchaser of this book or for quilts made for donation by the purchaser of this book for a non-profit group or organization. Care has been taken to ensure that the information and instructions herein are accurate but no warranty is provided nor results guaranteed. The author takes no responsibility or liability to any person or entity for loss or damage caused directly or indirectly from the information contained herein.

If there is a need for a correction in this book, it will be posted here: www.basilquilts.blog.com.

Creative Grids™ is a trademark of Creative Grids (UK) LTD.
Lil' Twister is a trademark of CS Designs (www.country-schoolhouse.com).

ISBN 978-0-692-45588-3
ISBN 13: 978-0-692-02-7936

First Edition

Also by Basil Papanastassiou, *Seven Simple Sensational Modern Quilts*

# Contents

# Introduction

## Preface

This book provides instruction on making ten modern quilts, simple in construction, and sophisticated in appearance. The patterns are suitable for the experienced beginner with the designs interesting enough for any quilter interested in modern quilting. For each quilt pattern I have also provided two alternate colorways to give you a sense as to how different fabrics affect the look of each quilt.

This book, while a "how to", is not an introduction to quilting. There are dozens of great books on the market that teach you how to quilt and experienced instructors that can show you all the steps to making quilts. The patterns in this book presume that you have already made a quilt or two, that you know how to sew a proper "scant ¼" seam", etc. Each of the quilts in this book is relatively simple to make without any complicated construction methods.

As with my first book, **Seven Simple Sensational Modern Quilts**, each of the patterns in this book is designed to be relatively easy to sew and to offer maximum visual impact. Each pattern can easily be made uniquely your own through the use of the fabric choices you make and each quilt can be made bigger or smaller simply by adjusting the amount of fabric you buy and how many blocks you make. Think of the patterns as inspirations for your own creativity and color combinations.

For the record, I designed and sewed all of the quilts in this book and had all quilts professionally quilted.

## Background

While finishing my first book, **Seven Simple Sensational Modern Quilts**, I figured I would be a one book wonder. I told myself that until I finished that book, I could not buy any more fabric or make another quilt. But then my local quilt shop got in the most amazing batik fabric and then, following one of my quilt philosophies (if you see it, buy it because when you go back for it, it won't be there), I bought it. It was too nice to cut up so I went home and designed a pattern that used full width of fabric panels. I finished the quilt in record time, brought it to my local quilt shop for quilting, and the owner asked if I would teach it at the store. This was June 2014 and I have taught the class three times so far and know of at least 36 fabric purchases to make that quilt, **In The Tropics** and it is the first quilt pattern in this book.

It appears I had at least one more book in me; I have presented the quilts in this book now to three different quilt guilds here in South Florida and have a waiting list of people interested in this book.

I am currently teaching five of these patterns locally and in each case, after the quilters make their first one, many of them went on to make at least one more using different fabrics. I love seeing the results.

## What Makes a Quilt Modern?

What makes a quilt "modern"? I think of modern quilting this way: new patterns and/or new fabrics or new interpretations of traditional patterns. This book shows examples, probably the best being **Modern Bargello** which interprets the traditional bargello pattern in bright solid colors, accented with black and white, and quilted using a modern quilt design.

In some cases, modern quilting relies on either updated quilting/stitching patterns or a quilt that shows what a talented and dedicated quilter can do when a quilt is actually machine or hand quilted.

## Tools/Supplies Needed

Just as a reminder, there are some basic supplies you need:

- **Sewing Machine with a Quarter-Inch Foot and a Sharp Needle**—You need a sewing machine in good working order with a quarter inch foot and optionally, a strip piecing guide. (A strip piecing guide is either removable tape or a channel that helps guide your fabric strips to help you achieve accuracy in sewing a quarter-inch seam.)
- **Walking Foot for your Sewing Machine**—Optional but helpful when sewing the binding onto your quilt is a walking foot.
- **Good Quality Cotton Thread**—Cheap thread is no bargain as it will break and/or generate a lot of dust and lint. I learned this lesson the hard way when I first started. If you are doing your own machine quilting, invisible polyester monofilament thread in either clear or smoke color is great for stitching in the ditch and tends to hide any imperfections in your quilting.
- **Rotary Cutter with a Sharp Blade**—Change your blade when you notice it skipping when cutting your fabric or when you notice it takes increasing pressure to make your cuts.
- **Self-Healing Cutting Mat**
- **Acrylic Rulers**—I recommend using a 6½" by 24½" and a large square ruler (helpful for squaring up fabric and blocks), and, optionally a 3½" by 12½" rectangular ruler (helpful for cutting strips into smaller pieces). I like the Creative Grids™ Non Slip rulers because they have non slip discs on the back to keep the ruler from sliding on the fabric while I am cutting it. For other brands of rulers you can buy little non-slip discs that are self-adhesive but, for me, the Creative Grids rulers are the best.
- **Iron and Ironing Board**
- **Scissors or a Pair of Snips for Trimming Threads**—I snip stray threads when I see them. Also, some fabrics tend to fray more than others (especially cheaper fabrics); if you don't catch a fraying thread early, it can continue to fray and any extraneous threads can eventually show through your quilt top when it is quilted.
- **Pins**—I like the "flat flower pins" which have a large flat head and are very thin and sharp and relatively inexpensive.
- **Seam Ripper**—Even I have to occasionally rip out a seam.
- **Wonder Clips by Clover**—These clips are great when sewing your bindings as they hold many layers of fabric. I use them to ensure that my binding is the same width on the front and back of my quilt and they hold so well I don't need to use pins. The base of the clip is flat so it feeds easily toward your sewing machine presser foot. I also use them to hold groups of quilt blocks together. They come in packs of 10, 50, and 100.
- **Accuracy**—Yes, I know accuracy is not technically a tool or supply but it is essential to creating a good quilt. You need to be accurate in cutting your fabric, in sewing a scant quarter inch seam (this is a seam that is just a little bit less than a quarter of an inch to allow for the thread when two pieces are sewn together), and in pressing. Any small deviation in cutting, sewing, and pressing will cause you problems when you sew your quilt together.

## General Pattern Notes

**Quarter Inch Seam Allowances Included in Pattern Pieces**—All pattern pieces include the quarter inch seam allowance in the dimensions.

**Fabric Width**—Instructions in this book are based upon fabric that is at least 42" wide. You may find some batiks are narrower and many fabrics wider but for purposes of estimating fabric, I have used 42" in width.

**Binding**—All pattern requirements allow sufficient fabric for 2½" width of fabric strips for binding.

**Backing Fabric and Batting**—The backing fabric and batting requirements listed for each pattern in this book add 12" total to the width and length of the quilt top. If you are having your quilts professionally quilted, check with your long arm quilter to see if he or she needs more or less than 12" total extra in width and length and if so, adjust the measurements accordingly.

**Multiple Strip Accuracy, Sewing**—When sewing together two or more strips along the long edges, it is important to pin the strips together every 6-8 inches to ensure that the strips do not stretch out of shape and to help you ensure that that they are feeding into your machine evenly.

Many machines feed the fabric under the presser foot just a smidgen more on the bottom than on the top and over a 42" length, can, without pinning, cause inaccuracies. Also, when sewing multiple strips together (anytime you sew two or more strips together it is called a strip set), reverse your starting point. In other words, sew one strip to another in one direction and when you go to sew the third strip, sew it on starting from the opposite end.

Sewing long strips together can cause them to begin to bow out and curve. If you reverse your direction when sewing, for example, a third strip to an already sewn group of two strips, you will help minimizing any potential for your strips to go out of alignment. This is also helpful when sewing rows and/or columns of strips together to prevent bowing of your rows and/or columns.

**Pressing**—When pressing your seams, it is important not to stretch your fabric. (Helpful hint: if stretching is an issue when pressing or sewing, use spray starch which helps to stabilize the fabric.) As in all quilting, you are pressing and not ironing, meaning you keep moving your iron across the fabric and setting it down to press your seams as opposed to running your iron across without lifting it up. It is helpful when sewing rows together to think about how you are going to press the blocks in the rows prior to actually pressing the rows.

If you press the seams in opposite directions from one row to the next row, it is easier to get the seams to nest together when pinning and sewing the rows together. This helps to align the seams so they match when you sew the rows together.

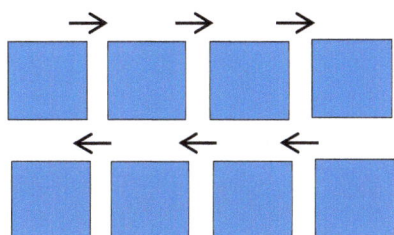

Obviously if you are going to be sewing a row of blocks to a piece of sashing it does not matter in which direction you press the seams of your blocks after sewing them into rows or columns. Note that if you are not careful when pressing, you can end up with fabric strips, pieces, blocks, or rows that are different sizes which can cause problems when sewing your quilt together.

**Border or No Border**—The choice of whether or not to include a border and, if so, what size and style is completely up to you. Each of the quilts in this book were designed with the border or no border decision in mind but each can be made with the borders as shown, with larger borders, or with no borders.

**Label Your Rows**—I always label the first block in my rows before I sew them together using a small piece of painter's tape—in the upper left-hand corner. This way I know which row is which, the orientation of the row (I have been known to sew the rows together upside down otherwise), and in which direction to press the seams between the blocks in the row. (I press the seams in the odd numbered blocks to the right and the seams in the even numbered blocks to the left.)

**Sewing Borders & Sashing**—When sewing your borders and long sashing strips, measure your quilt top before you cut your strips. For example, if you are sewing borders to the left and right sides of your quilt top, measure your quilt both at the top and bottom of your quilt; if the dimensions are not the same but off only slightly, take an average of these two measurements and cut your border strips to this average. Pin your border strip both at the top and bottom of your quilt top and then pin your border strip in the middle of your quilt top. Then pin in the middle between your quilt top and each end and then pin in the middle of those pins. This way your border and quilt top will be even. Since most sewing machines move the fabric very slightly differently between the feed dogs and the presser foot, multiple pins help ensure accurate border and sashing strip sewing.

**Backstitching Edges of Your Quilt Top**—The outside seams of your quilt top have the most stress on them when your quilt top is being quilted, especially if you are long arm quilting it or using someone else to quilt your quilts.

Therefore, it is best to either backstitch any seams that end at the outside edges of your quilt or sew a stitch 1/8" away from the outside edge of your quilt along the entire outside edge of your quilt top. This outside stitch will be hidden by your binding.

## Color/Fabric Selection

For those of you who have no trouble picking the right fabric for a quilt, you can either skip or skim this section. I have included alternate color options for each of the quilt patterns at the end of each chapter.

Feel free to replicate the quilts as shown or select your own fabrics. Some of the quilts in this book use solid colors surrounded by either white or black; some use prepackaged charm packs, and some were based on one or more "focus" fabrics—a special fabric that I bought because I liked the look of it and determined that I would eventually find a quilt pattern to highlight that fabric.

As I mentioned earlier, while I was finishing my first book, **Seven Simple Sensational Modern Quilts**, I saw an amazing batik which was too nice to cut into blocks but was perfect as the focus fabric for my **In The Tropics** pattern. (I have taught a class on this pattern a number of times and some of my students have gone on to make this same pattern using a variety of fabrics; all look amazing!)

In the quilt pattern **Focus on the Dove**, I used Fay Nicoll's Dove of Peace fabric (www.FayNicollJudaicaDesigns.com or www.SunshineSewing.com). For **Fast Focus Charms: Sea Life**, I used a fabric printed all over with five inch blocks which I then cut up to use as my focus fabric blocks. For **Fast Focus Fabric Blocks** I used a great print as the basis of the quilt (since half the quilt is made using one fabric) and picked three other fabrics that complemented that print.

I am always amazed at how different fabrics change the look of a quilt. The second quilt that I made would never have gotten made based upon the big picture the quilt designer/maker used in the illustration BUT there was also a smaller picture made of the same quilt using completely different fabrics which I really liked. (For that reason, I have included two different colorways for each of the quilts in this book.)

I am constantly having to remind myself when I look at a quilt pattern to imagine the quilt in different fabrics and then decide if I like the pattern or not. I was fortunate early on in my quilting when I went to a meeting of other quilters (a quilt guild) and fifteen of the guild had used the same pattern in making their quilts but each of the fifteen had used totally different fabrics. Some had used solid colors, some had used Asian-inspired fabrics, some had used traditional prints, and some had used modern prints. I was amazed at how different a quilt could look based solely on the fabrics that were used.

# Quilt Backs: Have Some Fun

Given the general interest about some of the more interesting things I have done on the back of my quilts, I have included a chapter on Quilt Backs and options for your quilt backs. Most quilts require joining at least two widths of fabric together. Depending on the quilt, I have used a variety of "designs"…

## Single Fabric Quilt Back

The easiest and simplest quilt back is two pieces of the same fabric sewn together to make the necessary width and length. To minimize the amount of fabric used on the back you can sew two widths together with a horizontal seam instead of a vertical seam

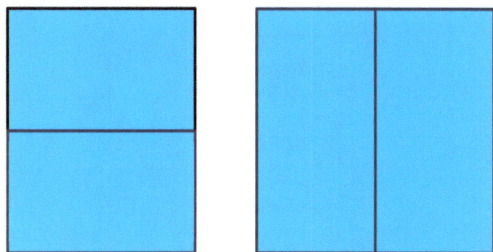

Since most quilting fabric is at least 42 inches wide, sewing two widths of fabric with a horizontal seam gives you at least 81 inches in length (typically you use ½" seams when sewing your quilt back) which is generally enough for most quilts. Some people prefer vertical seams which uses more fabric.

For example, for a quilt that is 60" by 72" and professionally quilted, my long arm quilter wants an additional 12" in width and 12" in length on the quilt back. So for the back of my 60" by 72" quilt, I need a quilt back that is 72" by 84". If I use a horizontal seam, I can buy 4 yards of fabric and sew a two yard piece to a two yard piece with a horizontal seam for my quilt back. (Generally quilt fabrics are more than 42" wide so after sewing the back with a horizontal seam, my back tends to be at least 84" long.

Now if use a vertical seam, to get the necessary length and width, I still need two pieces of fabric but each needs to be longer. Based upon that same 60" by 72" quilt with an additional 12"in width and 12"in length for my long arm quilter, I still need a back that measures 72" wide by 84" long. Therefore, I need two pieces that are each 84" long, or two pieces that are each $2^1/_3$ yards so I need a total of $4^2/_3$ yards. For comparison, on my 60" by 72" quilt back:

| Horizontal Seam | 4 yards |
| Vertical Seam | $4^2/_3$ yards |

With a vertical seam, you end up with extra width… Now if you plan to use the same fabric for your binding that you used on the back of your quilt, that extra width from sewing two widths of fabric together with a vertical seam can be used for your binding.

## Two Fabric Quilt Back

As long as you are going to have to have two widths of fabric in a typical quilt back, you can use two different fabrics.

Use two coordinating or contrasting fabrics cut the necessary length, cut one piece in half along the length of you're the fabric and sew the half width pieces on other side of your full width piece.

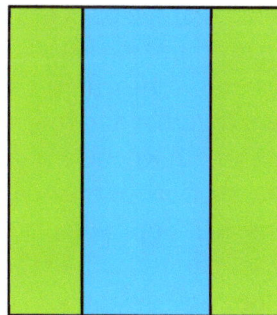

I have also used this same technique by taking a yard of fabric, cutting it to make two half yard pieces, sewing them together to make one piece 18" by 84" and then using that as the

center back on a quilt. (Since I occasionally have a one yard piece of fabric that I bought with the intention of using it "someday", using it on the back of a quilt allows me to use that fabric.)

## Center Panel on the Back

Sometimes I will take a yard of fabric and make it the center of a quilt back with a contrasting or coordinating fabric surrounding the yard. Since a yard of fabric is 36" by 42", it makes a nice big center block on the back of the quilt:

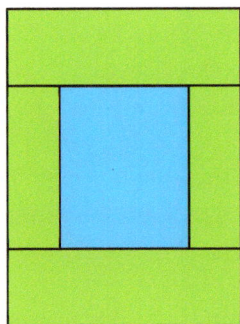

I have successfully used a patterned fabric as the center panel with a coordinating solid around it—very modern and it makes the quilt reversible!

## Leftover Quilt Top Fabric

Use any fabric leftover from making your quilt top on the back.

For example, when I made the **Modern Bargello** quilt, I had the colored pieces that made the bargello left over so I sewed them together as the center column of the back of the quilt. The pieces were already the same length as the length of the colored vertical pieces so it was easy to sew them together and they were exactly the same length when sewn as the colored strips on the front of the quilt. (I did have to sew some black to the top and bottom of the back to allow for the extra 12" in length needed for my long arm quilter but I used the black fabric that was trimmed after quilting to make my binding.)

Again, it makes the quilt very modern, looks like a different quilt on the back, and I used up the remaining colored fabrics from the front of

the quilt. Also the quilting pattern really stood out on the black fabric as the quilter used white fabric in the bobbin.

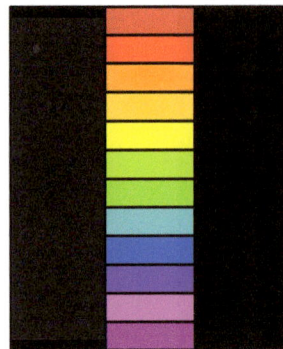

In my **Fast Focus Fabric Blocks** quilt, since I had pulled all the fabrics from my stash, I had fabric leftover. So I took the three fabrics I used for my rail fence blocks and sewed them together into repeating strips centered between the leftover focus fabric.

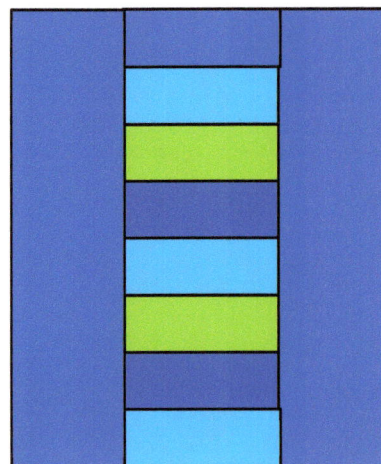

## Leftover Quilt Blocks

Sometimes there are blocks leftover from your quilt top. Incorporate them into the back of your quilt. For example, with the **Positive/Negative** quilt, I had four blocks left over. I sewed them together and incorporated them in the center of the back of the quilt and used more of the neutral fabric from the front of the quilt to surround them. It made a striking back.

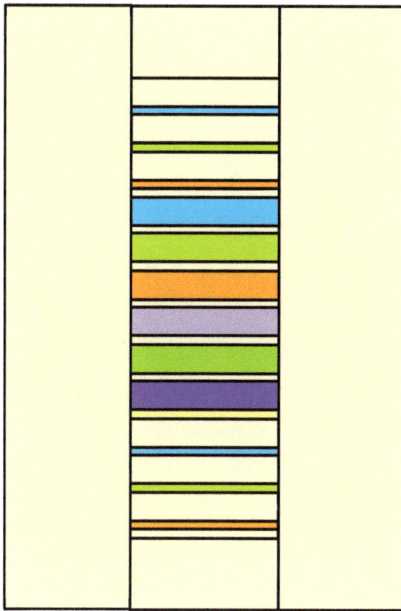

## Wide Back Fabrics

Some fabric companies make wide back fabric—instead of the normal 42-44" wide fabrics, they make the fabric 102-115" wide. This means if you find a wide back fabric you like, you can buy enough yardage for your back without having to sew anything together. These wide back fabrics are marketed as "wide quilt backing", "widebacks", "quilt backing", "quilt backing fabric", and "quilt fabric wide back".

Once in a while you get lucky. I was making a quilt and waited until I had pieced and sewn the quilt top before selecting/buying the border fabric. I found the perfect wide back fabric for the quilt and since the fabric was 108" wide, I bought enough yardage for the quilt back and since I did not need 108" for the length of my quilt, cut my borders from this wider back fabric piece as well.

# In The Tropics

61½" by 69½"

This quilt is designed to highlight a focus fabric. It has become the most popular quilt pattern I have ever designed and taught. It calls for five panels of the focus fabric cut the full width of the fabric, braid constructed from 2½" strips, and sashing. For those unfamiliar with braids, Creative Grids™ makes a terrific ruler (Creative Grids 45° Trapezoid Strip Ruler) that simplifies the cutting of the specific shapes that make up the braid (called trapezoids). Once you cut the trapezoids from 2½" width of fabric strips, it is relatively easy to sew a braid together. Simply pick a focus fabric you really like, either find a jellyroll that complements it or buy some complementary fabric, and sew an amazing quilt.

## Fabric Requirements

| Focus Fabric | 1¾ yards |
| --- | --- |
| Sashing | ⅝ yard |
| Braid | 30 2½" width of fabric strips (or 10 ¼ yards cut into 2½" strips) |
| Binding | ⅝ yard (exactly 7 2½" strips) |
| Back | 4 yards for a horizontal seam, 4⅔ yards for a vertical seam (includes additional 12" in width and length for long arm quilting) |
| Batting | 73" by 82" |

Required: Creative Grids™ 45° Trapezoid Strip Ruler
Optional: Spinning 17" Cutting Mat for ease in cutting the trapezoids

## Construction

1. **Cut your focus fabric panels.** From your focus fabric, cut five pieces 11½" by the width of fabric. Trim the selvedges off the pieces and cut two focus fabric panel pieces to 44" long and two focus fabric panel pieces to 36 ½" long; set them aside. The fifth piece will be used for the middle focus fabric panel. (Note: for fabric 42" wide, cut two focus fabric panel pieces to 42" long.)

2. **Cut or select your braid strips.** IF using precut strips, skip to Step 3. IF using your own fabrics, cut thirty (30) 2½" by width of fabric strips from a variety of fabrics.

3. **Cut your 2½" width of fabric strips into trapezoids.** Keeping each 2½"strip folding in half, wrong side to wrong side, position the 45° Trapezoid Strip Ruler on top of the selvedge ends and trim off the selvedges.

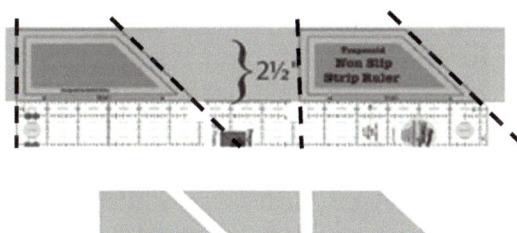

Without moving the ruler, cut the three trapezoid shapes from your folded strip. (With practice and a sharp blade in your rotary cutter, you can cut multiple strips simultaneously.) Shift the ruler over the rest of your strip(s) and cut an additional set of trapezoids. Lift the ruler off your strip(s) and separate the pieces into two piles: the top pieces in one pile (right-hand trapezoids) and the bottom pieces turned right-side up in another pile (left-side trapezoids). Cut all fabric strips keeping the piles of the same color together and the same orientation of the angle cuts together. If after cutting your first set of trapezoids the leftover folded piece is large enough, press it to remove the fold and cut another trapezoid from it. Some fabrics are wider than others—you may not be able to make an additional trapezoid from every strip. (Note: The Creative Grid Trapezoid ruler includes a small instruction sheet if you need more information on cutting the braid pieces.)

4. **Decide how to arrange the different fabrics in your braid.** Arrange your trapezoids in a random fashion into two piles: left-hand trapezoids and right-hand trapezoids.

Left- hand and right-hand pieces

Right sides together, stitch at short edge

Open and finger press down

Add 3<sup>rd</sup> piece repeat steps

5. **Sew your braid**. Refer to the diagram on the following page. Take one left-hand and one right-hand trapezoid. Lay the right-hand trapezoid on top of the left-hand trapezoid, right sides together, and sew them together along the top right-hand edge. Finger press seams toward the angles. Place another left-hand piece on top of the two you have sewn and sew that piece along the long side; match the top 90 degree ends as the two angled ends will not match when sewing but will match when you open up the pieces. Sew a right-hand piece onto what you have already sewn. Continue to process of sewing left- and right-hand pieces one by one to form a long braid. Press seams towards the open angle every one to two feet; you do not have to press every seam after sewing. After sewing the first foot or so of braid, check your braid's width: it should measure exactly six inches wide. If it is a little wider, later on trim it to six inches.

NOTE: Since the quilt has pieces at the edges of the quilt (as opposed to a border), you need to either back stitch your braid pieces to ensure that your quilt does not begin to come apart especially when it is long arm quilted OR instead of back stitching each piece of your braid, when you finish your quilt top, you can sew a seam 1/8" from the edge of your quilt around the outside of your quilt top.

6. **Continue sewing your braid**. Continue sewing your braid until you have used all your trapezoid pieces; you need twenty-eight feet of braid to make this quilt. (OPTIONAL: After sewing about eight feet of braid, jump ahead and make up one of the four main panels of the quilt. Refer to Step 8, below. )

7. **Cut your sashing pieces**. From your sashing fabric, cut twelve 1½" width of fabric strips. Cut six to 44" long (or 42" long if your focus fabric is only 42" wide and you cut two focus fabric pieces to 42" long) and six to 36½" long.

8. **Cut four 44" (or 42" if your focus fabric is only 42" wide) braid lengths for the left- and right-hand side focus fabric panels**. Trim the angled end of your braid to square it up. Cut four 44" (or 42" if your focus fabric is only 42" wide) long pieces. Note: There is sufficient braid so you can determine where you want to make your cuts so you can pick the parts of the braid you want in your quilt.

9. **Make two braid/sashing/focus fabric panels for the left and right sides of your quilt**. Make two 44" (or 42" if your focus fabric is only 42" wide) braid/sashing/focus fabric panels for the left- and right-sides of your quilt. (IF your focus fabric and/or sashing fabric is shorter after trimming your selvedge edges, use that length.) Sew one braid to one sashing strip and press the seams toward the sashing strip. Sew the braid/sashing strip, to the fabric panel with the sashing strip between the braid and the focus fabric panel. Press the seams toward the sashing strip. Sew the second sashing strip to the second braid making sure that

two braids are going in the same direction. Press the seams toward the sashing strip. Sew the sashing strip/braid unit to the focus fabric panel and press towards the sashing strip. You now have one of the four main sections of the quilt done. Admire your work. Repeat to make a second 44" (or 42") braid/sashing/focus fabric panel.

10. **Make two 36½" braid/sashing/focus fabric panels for the top and bottom of your quilt.** Follow instructions in Steps 8 and 9 to make two additional braid/sashing/ focus fabric panels for the top and bottom of your quilt that measure 36½" long.

11. **Trim the last width of fabric piece for the center of the quilt.** From the last 11½" by width of fabric panel, trim the length to 19". (If your focus fabric was 42" wide, trim the last width to 17".)

12. **Determine the arrangement of your four braid panels.** The braids on the left- and right-side 44" long panels can either both be angled up or angled down or one angled up and one angled down. The top and bottom 36½" braid panels can have the braids angled left or right. Determine the positioning of all four panels. Sew a sashing strip to the right-hand side of the left-hand vertical panel and to the left side of the right-hand vertical panel. Sew a sashing strip to the bottom of the top braid panel and sew a sashing strip to the top of bottom braid panel. Press seams toward the sashing strips.

13. **Sew your quilt top pieces together.** Using the diagram that follows, sew focus fabric piece 2 to piece 1 and then press towards the sashing strip. Sew piece 3 to pieces 1 and 2

and press the seams toward the sashing strip. Sew piece 5 next to pieces 2 and 3 and press the seams toward the sashing strip. Sew piece 4 to the rest of the quilt:

On the back of piece 4 where it will meet pieces 1 and 2, place a visible mark ¼" away from the corner on both left-side and bottom edges. On the back of the pieces 1 and 2, place a visible mark ¼" away from the corner on both right-side and top edges.

When pinning piece 4 to the rest of the quilt, make sure you line up the marks you made—so you can sew piece 4 into the rest of the quilt and end up with a perfect seam at the intersection of pieces 1, 2, and 5. Sew the first seam and when the sewing machine needle is at the marks you made, stop sewing and with the needle in the down position, lift the presser foot, turn the fabric in the direction you need to sew, lower the presser foot, and sew your last seam in your quilt top. Press seams toward the sashing.

14. **Trim any loose threads and, if necessary, square up your quilt top.** If you did not back stitch each braid piece when sewing your braid together, sew a line of stitching 1/8" from the edge of your quilt top all the way around to stabilize the quilt prior to quilting (it keeps the individual pieces from coming unstitched when the quilt is quilted).

15. **Sew your back together and either quilt it or deliver it to your long arm quilting service.**

16. **Bind your quilt.** Sew seven 2½" wide with of fabric strips together for your binding and then bind your quilt.
17. **Make and sew a label onto your quilt. Enjoy!**

Note: if your focus fabric was only 42" wide, your quilt will be two inches shorter; the instructions above note where you would need to make changes to your fabric cutting.

## Color Options

Many of my students opted to make a second (and in some cases a third or fourth) version of this quilt. I have reproduced their color choices below to give you some ideas as to other color variations. Both large focus panels were prints—the blue being a large floral and the grey being a large repeating pattern. In each case, once the focus fabric was chosen, the colors in the focus fabric were used in the braids. Trust me, the finished quilts look great!

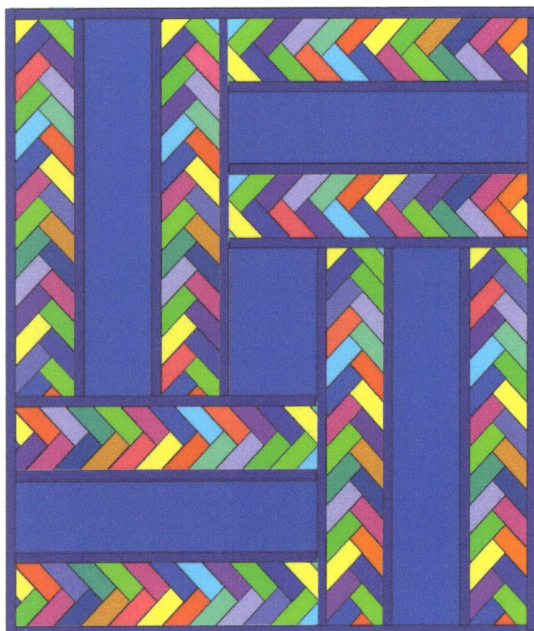

# Modern Bargello

Finished quilt 50" by 60"

A bargello quilt is one with fabric strips sewn together then subcut and resewn, offsetting the individual colors to create movement. In this case I offset the traditional bargello pattern with black and white to create a secondary pattern. This quilt is very bold but lends itself to a variety of color options. Any group of twelve fabrics plus black and white will work. I made mine as a wall hanging but have included fabric requirements and instructions to make the same pattern as a throw—it is exactly the same construction but using slightly bigger pieces of fabric.

## Fabric Requirements

|  | Wall Hanging (50" by 60") | Throw (50" by 72") |
|---|---|---|
| Black Fabric | 1⅓ yards | 1½ yards |
| White Fabric | ⅔ yards | ¾ yards |
| Colored Fabric | 12 ⅙ yards of 12 different colors OR two 2½" width of fabric strips of 12 different colors | 12 ¼ yards of 12 different colors OR two 2½" width of fabric strips of 12 different colors |
| Binding | ½ yard | ½ yards |
| Backing fabric | 3½ yards for horizontal seams, 4 yards for vertical seams (includes additional 12" in width and length for long arm quilting) | 3½ yards for horizontal seams, 4⅔ yards for vertical seams (includes additional 12" in width and length for long arm quilting) |
| Batting | 62" x 72" | 62" x 84" |

## Construction

The instructions are for making a 50" x 60" wall hanging or a 50" x 72" throw. Changes needed for the 50" x 72" version are shown in brackets.

1. **Cut your black fabric strips.** From the black fabric cut two pieces 20½" by width of fabric. Subcut these into 26 pieces 2½" by 20½". [For throw, cut two black fabric pieces 24½" by width of fabric. Subcut these into 26 2½" by 24½" pieces.]

2. **Cut your white fabric strips.** From the white fabric trim the fabric to 20½" by width of fabric. Subcut this into 13 pieces 2½" by 20½". [For throw, trim the fabric to 24½" by width of fabric. Subcut this into 13 pieces 2½" by 24½".]

3. **Make six strip sets from the colored (non black or white) fabrics.** Trim each of your twelve colored fabrics to 5½" by width of fabric. Make six strip sets as follows: sew the red to the red/orange pieces along the long sides, sew orange to the orange/yellow, yellow to the yellow green, green to the green/blue, blue to the blue/purple, and purple to the purple/red. Press the seams open. [For the throw, trim each of your twelve colored fabrics to 6½" by width of fabric and follow the same instructions.] For example:

4. **Cut twelve strips from each of the paired fabrics.** For each of the twelve strip sets from Step 3, trim off the selvedge from one side and cut twelve 2½" wide strips. The extra left over from cutting the twelve pieces can be used for the back of your quilt. [For the throw, same instructions.]

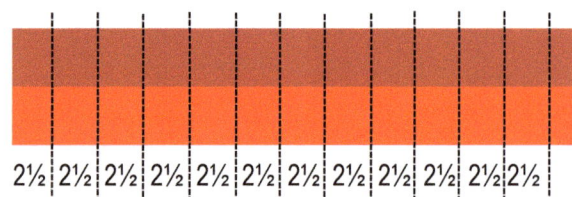

2½ 2½ 2½ 2½ 2½ 2½ 2½ 2½ 2½ 2½ 2½ 2½

5. **Sew your colored strips columns.** You are going to sew twelve paired strips from Step 4, six groups of two sets of strips, for four colors in each strip:

   a. Sew the red & red/orange to the orange & orange/yellow strips at the short ends. Repeat so you have two of them. Press the seams open.

b. Sew the yellow & yellow/green and green & green/blue strips together at the short ends. Repeat so you have two of them. Press the seams open.

c. Sew the blue and blue/purple and the purple and purple/red strips together at the short ends. Repeat so you have two of them. Press the seams open.

6. **Sew the first two colored columns.** This sounds more complicated than it really is—just read through the directions before you start to sew. You are going to be sewing two columns from the four-piece strips you created in Step 5 (refer to the diagram that follows). Sew a red | red orange | orange | orange yellow strip to a yellow | yellow green | green | green blue strip to a blue | blue purple | purple | purple red strip. Repeat. Press seams open. Now remove the red piece from the end of one strip and sew it to the purple/red end of the other strip. These are the first two colored columns in your quilt!

7. **Repeat Step 6 following the diagram with the other columns.**

8. **Sew 13 black/white/black columns.** Take the long black pieces and long white pieces from

Steps 1 and 2 and sew 13 sets of black/white/black strips by sewing the short ends together. Press toward the black strips.

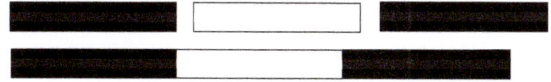

9. **Sew the black/white/black columns to the colored strips.** Following the diagram that follows the instructions, sew the columns together, alternating a black/white/black strip with a colored strip, paying attention to the order of the colored strips. Press seams toward the colored strips (this avoids any of the colored strips showing through from the back of the white pieces.

The first and last columns should be black/white/black columns. Make sure to alternate the direction of your sewing when sewing your columns together; this helps your quilt top stay square.

10. **Sew reinforcing stiches.** Before your quilt top can be quilted, sew a line of stiches across the top and bottom of your quilt, approximately 1/8" from the edge. This helps avoid the columns of your quilt top separating as it is stretched in the quilt frame of a long arm quilting machine.

11. **Seam your backing fabric and prepare your quilt top for quilting.** Trim any loose threads, square up your quilt top, and cut and seam

together your backing fabric. Make sure your quilt top is properly pressed and square. *Optional*: I used the leftover colored pieces as the center of the back of my quilt (see page 6): trim the pieces so they are all the same width and sew them together into one column starting with the red and ending with the red/purple piece. Sew fabric to either side of your column to complete your back. I added additional fabric to the top and bottom of my color column to allow for quilting (the people who do my quilting want an additional 8-12" in total width and length on my quilt back to help in pinning the back

fabric onto the quilt frame and layering the quilt top and batting onto it.

12. **Layer your backing fabric, batting, and quilt top together and quilt it OR deliver them to your long arm quilter.**

13. **After quilting, trim the quilt so that it is square and bind it.** The fabric requirements allow for six 2½" strips cut from the width of the fabric. [Throw: seven 2½" strips.]

14. **Enjoy your new quilt!** I did not want to end up with only thirteen steps in case someone was superstitious.

## Color Options

Here are some other options for your quilt. I showed one with a border and one without to give you some ideas.

# Fast Focus Fabric Blocks

Finished Quilt 54½" by 66½", Finished block 6" square, 9 blocks x 11 blocks

This is an updated version of a classic quilt pattern and incredibly fast to make as half of the quilt is your focus fabric cut into 6½" squares! This quilt is also easy to make bigger or smaller as the finished size of each block is 6" square. There are only two different blocks in this quilt: your focus fabric square and a strip pieced three strip square. Pick a focus fabric that you love and three coordinating fabrics and you are ready to go. Because each strip set makes five blocks and each width of focus fabric strip makes five blocks, it is relatively easy to make a larger or smaller quilt.

## Fabric Requirements

| Focus Fabric | 1⅓ yards |
|---|---|
| Coordinating Fabrics | 3 fabrics, ⅔ yard each |
| Binding | ½ yard |
| Backing fabric | 3¾ yards for horizontal seams, 4½ yards for vertical seams (includes additional 12" in length and width to allow for long arm quilting) |
| Batting | 66" x 78" (includes additional 12" in length and width to allow for long arm quilting) |

## Construction

1. **Cut your focus fabric blocks.** From your focus fabric, cut nine 6½" width of fabric strips. From each of these strips, cut six 6½" squares. You need 50 squares; four are extra.

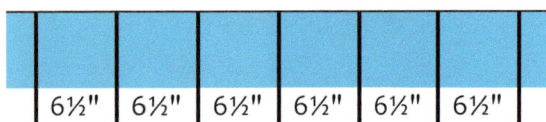

| 6½" | 6½" | 6½" | 6½" | 6½" | 6½" |
|---|---|---|---|---|---|

2. **Cut your coordinating fabric into 2½"width of fabric strips.** For each of the three coordinating fabrics, cut nine 2½"width of fabric strips.

3. **Sew nine three-fabric strip sets.** Sew together three strips, one of each color. (This is called a strip set.) Press the seams toward the darkest fabric. Repeat until you have sewn nine strip sets

4. **Cut your strip sets into 6½" squares.** Trim off the selvedge from one end and cut six 6½" squares from each strip sets. You will end up with 54 squares (five are extra).

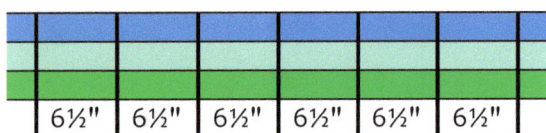

| 6½" | 6½" | 6½" | 6½" | 6½" | 6½" |
|---|---|---|---|---|---|

5. **Sew your blocks into rows.** Refer to either the picture at the beginning of this section or the diagram that follows to sew your blocks together into rows. There are nine blocks in each row. For the first row and last row, backstitch the block intersections at the outside edge, that is, the edge that will end up on the perimeter of your quilt. The backstitching helps ensure that your blocks in the perimeter do not begin to separate. Press the seams in opposite directions in each row to help ensure that your quilt top stays straight. (I press the odd-numbered row seams to the right and the even numbered row seams to the left—this helps when sewing the rows together as the seams "nest" together. There are eleven rows.

6. **Sew your rows together.** Refer to either the picture at the beginning of this section or the diagram that follows to sew each of your quilt rows together. Match the seams from one row to the next and pin as necessary. Backstitch at the beginning and end of each row. Alternate the direction in which you sew the rows together, for example, sewing rows 1 and 2 together from left to right and then sewing rows 2 and 3 together from right to left. This also helps to ensure your quilt remains even and "square".

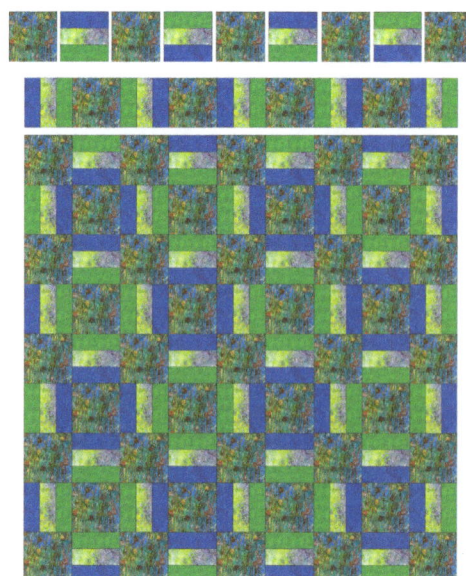

7. **Seam your backing fabric and prepare your quilt top for quilting.** Trim any loose threads, square up your quilt top, and cut and seam together your backing fabric. Make sure your quilt top is properly pressed and square.

8. **Layer your backing fabric, batting, and quilt top together and quilt it OR deliver them to your long arm quilter.**

9. **After quilting, trim the quilt so that it is square and bind it.** The fabric requirements allow for seven 2½" strips cut from the width of the fabric.

10. **Enjoy your new quilt and marvel at how fast this quilt came together!**

## Color Options

The large scale of the blocks and strips allow great flexibility as shown below:

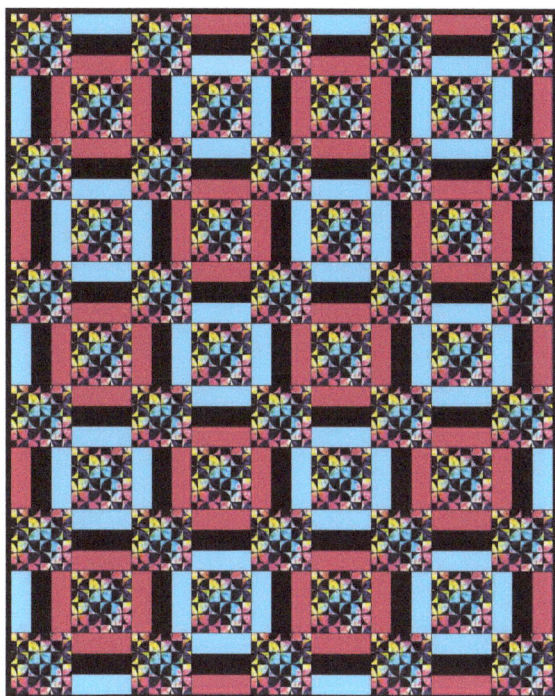

# Fast Focus Charms: Sea Life

Finished Quilt 58½" by 67½", Finished block 4½" square, 11 blocks x 13 blocks

This is an updated version of a classic quilt pattern and incredibly fast to make as half of the quilt is your focus fabric cut into 5" squares! This quilt is also easy to make bigger or smaller as the finished size of each block is 4½" square. There are only two different blocks in this quilt: your focus fabric and a strip pieced three strip square. Pick a focus fabric that you love or a panel with squares that you can cut into 5" squares, three coordinating fabrics, and you are ready to go.

Because each strip set makes eight blocks and each width of focus fabric strip makes eight blocks, it is relatively easy to make a larger or smaller quilt.

## Fabric Requirements

| Focus Fabric | 1⅓ yards if using a focus fabric with individual squares; if using a focus fabric that you cut into 5" squares, you need 1½ yards OR you can use 2 packages of charm squares for a more scrappy look |
|---|---|
| Coordinating Fabrics | 3 fabrics, 1 yard each for blocks and borders; if using charm square packages, pick three fabrics that coordinate with the charm squares. Note: if you want to use your focus fabric for both squares and borders, you need 1⅓ yards of a focus fabric for your 5" squares and 2 yards of fabric for borders and binding. |
| Binding | ½ yard |
| Backing fabric | 4½ yards for a vertical seam, 4 yards for a horizontal seam (includes additional 12" in length and width to allow for long arm quilting) |
| Batting | 70" x 80" (includes additional 12" in length and width to allow for long arm quilting) |

## Construction

1. **Cut your focus fabric blocks.** You need 76 5" squares. (Four squares are the corner blocks in your borders.)

   If using prepacked charm squares, you need 76 squares; skip to the next step.

   If using the Sea Life panel, fussy cut 76 5" squares. If using a focus fabric, cut ten 5" width of fabric strips and then subcut those into 5" squares; four are extra.

   If using a single focus fabric, cut nine 5" width of fabric strips and subcut these into 5" squares.

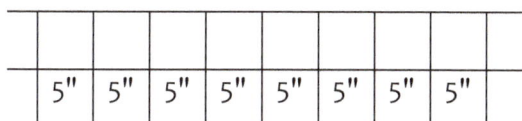

   | | | | | | | | |
   |---|---|---|---|---|---|---|---|
   | 5" | 5" | 5" | 5" | 5" | 5" | 5" | 5" |

2. **Cut your coordinating fabric into 2" width of fabric strips.** For each of the three coordinating fabrics, cut nine 2"width of fabric strips.

3. **Sew nine three-fabric strip sets.** Sew together three strips, one of each color. (This is called a strip set.) Press the seams toward the darkest fabric.

4. **Cut your strip sets into 5" squares.** Trim off the selvedge from one end and cut eight 5" squares from each strip sets. You will end up with 72 squares (one is extra).

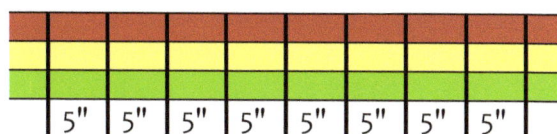

5. **Sew your blocks into rows.** Refer to either the picture at the beginning of this section or the diagram that follows to sew your blocks together into rows. There are 11 blocks in each row. Press the seams in opposite directions in each row to help ensure that your quilt top stays straight. (I press the odd-numbered row seams to the right and the even numbered row seams to the left—this helps when sewing the rows together as the seams "nest" together.) There are thirteen rows.

6. **Sew your rows together.** Refer to either the picture at the beginning of this section or the diagram that follows to sew each of your quilt rows together. Match the seams from one row to the next and pin as necessary. Backstitch at the beginning and end of each row. Alternate the direction in which you sew the rows together, for example, sewing rows 1 and 2 together from left to right and then sewing rows 2 and 3 together from right to left. This also helps to ensure your quilt remains even and "square". (You may think that this is unnecessary but in one of my

classes, a student chose to ignore this recommendation and by the end of the quilt, there was a slight but definite curve at the bottom of the quilt.)

7. **Seam fabric for your borders.** Cut six 2" strips from each of your three coordinating fabrics. Sew three strips from one of the fabrics end to end to end to make one very long strip. Repeat with the other strips and other coordinated fabrics until you have two very long strips of each color. Now sew two strip sets using the three colors; note that the order of the colors is different from your blocks in that what was the middle color is now the outside color. In the sample quilt, the order of colors in the blocks was red cream green; for the border, the order is red green cream.

Offset the start of each of the three strips from each other so this way the seams of the three strips are separated from each other; this helps the look of your quilt. Offset the strips by four to six inches is sufficient.

Note: if you are using a single coordinating fabric for your border, cut four 5½" length of fabric strips and use these strips for your border; the rest of the fabric, cut the length of the fabric, can be used for your binding.

8. **Measure your quilt top and cut your border strips.** Measure the top and bottom of your quilt; they should be the same and write this measurement down. Measure the left and right sides of your quilt; they should be the same and write this measurement down. If your measurements top and bottom or left and right are not the same, check your pressing and/or seam allowances and make whatever changes are needed to square up your quilt. From each long strip set, cut two pieces the size of the width of your quilt top and the length of your quilt top.

9. **Attach your borders to your quilt top.** Sew the long border strips to the left and right sides of your quilt top and press the seams toward the borders. Attach the four

cornerstone blocks you saved to each end of the top and bottom border strips and sew them to your quilt top; press the seams toward the borders.

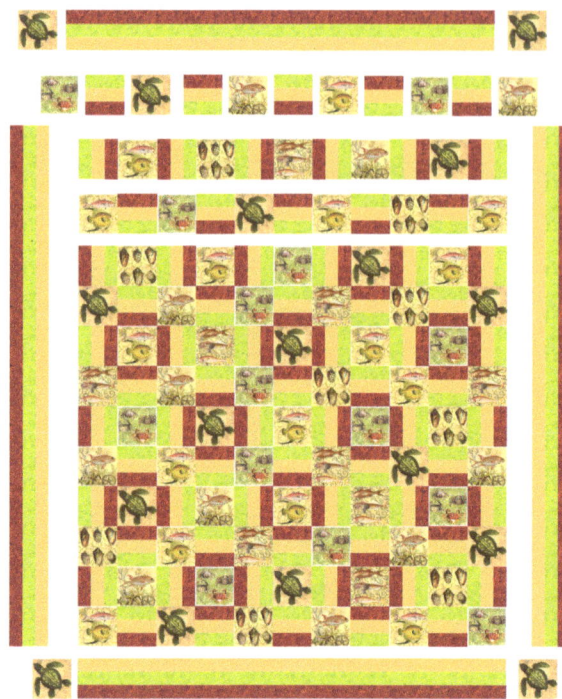

10. **Seam your backing fabric and prepare your quilt top for quilting.** Trim any loose threads, square up your quilt top, and cut and seam together your backing fabric. Make sure your quilt top is properly pressed and square.

11. **Layer your backing fabric, batting, and quilt top together and quilt it OR deliver them to your long arm quilter.**

12. **After quilting, trim the quilt so that it is square and bind it.** The fabric requirements allow for seven 2½" strips cut from the width of the fabric.

13. **Enjoy your new quilt and marvel at how fast this quilt came together!**

14. **Make another using your favorite focus fabric.** For those who are superstitious, I added an optional Step 14.

# Color Options

You can easily vary the look of this quilt either by using charm packs or a single focus fabric.

# Sprinkles

Finished quilt 48" x 60" Finished block 6" square, 8 blocks x 10 blocks

This is a happy quilt made up of a background fabric and thin strips of bright colors. It reminds me of the rainbow sprinkles you use to decorate ice cream sundaes and cakes. It is easy to make bigger or smaller as each strip set makes 5 blocks. A number of my students have made multiple versions of this quilt, not only using a light background fabric but also other versions using dark patterned background fabrics with great results. I show two other examples at the end of this chapter.

## Fabric Requirements

| Background Fabric | 3¾ yards |
|---|---|
| Accent Fabrics | Eight colors, ⅛ yard each |
| Binding | ½ yard |
| Backing Fabric | 3⅓ yards with a horizontal seam, 4 yards for a vertical seam (allows an additional 12" in both width and length to allow for professional long arm quilting) |
| Batting | 60" x 72" (allows an additional 12" in both width and length to allow for professional long arm quilting) |

## Construction

1. **Cut your accent color strips**. Cut two 2" by width of fabric strips from each of your eight accent color fabrics.

2. **Cut your background fabric strips**. Cut 32 4" by width of fabric strips from your background fabric.

3. **Sew 16 strip sets together**. Sew three strips together across the length of the strips, the background fabric on the outsides and a colored strip in the middle. Sew 16 sets, eight sets each with two of the same color in the middle. When sewing the strips together, alternate the direction in which you sew—this helps keep the strip set straight. (You may think this is unnecessary but in one of my classes, a student ignored this instruction and her strip sets ended up with a slight curve.) Press the seams toward the colored strip (this way the color won't show through your quilt top).

4. **Cut your strip sets into blocks**. Take a large 6½" wide ruler that has a 30/60 degree line on it and align the 30 degree line on the bottom edge of your strip set as shown on the diagram below. (NOTE: Do not use the 45 degree angle line.). Cut on both sides of your strip set. Move the ruler along to the right and align the 30/60 degree line along the bottom edge of your strip set and the left side of the ruler along your cut edge and cut the right edge of your strip set. Continue along your strip set; you will get 5 strips from

each of your strip sets. Repeat with all 16 strip sets.

5. **Cut your strips from Step 4 into blocks**. Using a 6½" wide ruler, cut each of your "blocks" from Step 4 into 6½" wide squares.

6. **Arrange your blocks eight blocks by ten blocks**. Determine how you want to lay out your blocks; there are a variety of ways from random to the alternating squares and pinwheel effect shown on the diagram that follows.

7. **Sew your blocks into rows**. Sew your blocks into rows. Press the seams in the odd numbered rows to the right and press the seams in the even numbered rows to the left. This way when you sew the rows to each other, you can nest the seams between the

blocks to help ensure that your blocks intersect and line up properly.

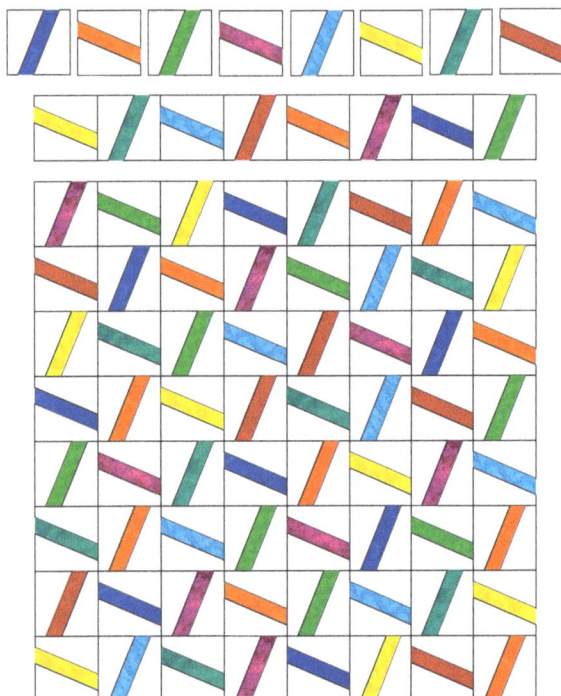

8. **Sew your rows together**. Sew your rows together alternating the direction in which you press the seams to help ensure the quilt top stays straight and square. This also helps to ensure your quilt remains even and "square". (You may think that this is unnecessary but in one of my classes, a student chose to ignore this recommendation and by the end of the quilt, there was a slight but definite curve at the bottom of the quilt.)

9. **Seam your backing fabric and prepare your quilt top for quilting**. Trim any loose threads, square up your quilt top, and cut and seam together your backing fabric. Make sure your quilt top is properly pressed and square.

10. **Layer your backing fabric, batting, and quilt top together and quilt it OR deliver them to your long arm quilter.**

11. **After quilting, trim the quilt so that it is square and bind it**. The fabric requirements allow for six 2½" strips cut from the width of the fabric.

Note: Each strip set makes five blocks and each block finishes at 6" square. If you want to make your quilt bigger, it is relatively easy to figure out how much additional fabric you need. For example, to increase the size of the quilt from the illustrated 48" by 60" to 60" by 72", you would need to add 2 blocks in width to each row and 2 blocks in length to each column. A 48" by 60" quilt is 80 blocks arranged 8 blocks by 10 blocks for a total of 80 blocks. A 60" by 72" quilt is 10 blocks by 12 blocks for a total of 120 blocks or a fifty percent increase in size and therefore you would need 50% more fabric.

For each set of 10 blocks you need *exactly* 16" by width of fabric of background fabric and 4" of colored accent fabric. (When increasing the size of your quilt, one of the easiest ways is to add additional colors to those in the basic quilt or repeat some of your favorite colors from your basic palette.)

## Color Options

In the classes I taught on this quilt, many choose to make a second (and in one case a third) version of this quilt. Below are two variations. Notice how simply changing the background fabric to black gives the quilt a completely different appearance. The second version is very "masculine" with a tan background and only two colors: blue and brown.

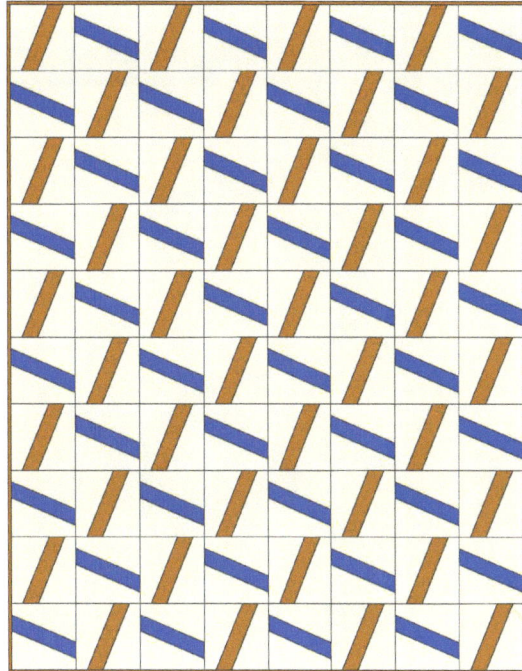

# Big Modern Braid

54" by 68"

This modern take on the traditional braid uses a simple innovate method to create the braid from large strip sets you then cut easily into the "trapezoidal" shape for the braid—no trimming the edges to create the braid shape! Each of the brightly colored fabrics above is in the shape of a trapezoid; my method simplifies the process of cutting these shapes without the need to trim the sides of your braid after sewing it together.

## Fabric Requirements

| Braid Fabrics | • ⅛ yard each of ten fabrics for wide braids (or any combination of ten 3" width of fabric strips) |
| | • ½ yards each of two contracting fabrics used on either side of wide braid strips |
| Border Fabrics | Outside Border: 1⅔ yards (used for binding too) |
| | Inner Border: ⅓ yard |
| Binding: | Included in fabric requirement for outside border |
| Backing Fabric | 4½ yards for vertical seams; 3¾ yards for horizontal seams (includes additional 12" in both width and length to allow for long arm quilting) |
| Batting | 66"x80" (includes additional 12" in both width and length to allow for long arm quilting) |

## Construction

1. **Cut your braid strips.** From each of your ten wide braid fabrics, cut one 3" by width of fabric strip. From each of your two contrasting narrow braid fabrics, cut ten 1½" width of fabric strips.

2. **Sew 10 braid fabric strips.** For each of your ten 3" by width of fabric strips, sew one light and one dark narrow braid fabric strip to each side of your 3" by width of fabric strips. Press toward the darker strips. Note: to help stabilize the fabric prior to cutting and sewing, it is helpful to press using a spray starch.

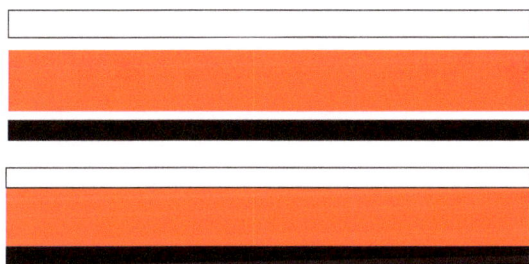

3. **Cut each braid strip set into three 14" pieces.** Trim off the selvedge from one end of each braid strip set and trim the strip set into three 14" long pieces. You should have thirty 14" long pieces.

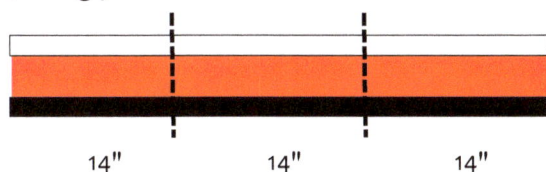

14"      14"      14"

4. **Cut your braid trapezoids.** Place two of the same 14" strips right sides together and place on your cutting mat, aligning the bottom left-hand sides with the "0" on your mat; the right-hand bottom corner should align with the 14" marking on your mat. Using your acrylic ruler, align the ruler's 45 degree line with the bottom horizontal "0" line with the bottom right-hand corner on the 9½" space on the mat (refer to the diagram below). Cut along the right-hand edge of the ruler to cut your strips into two pieces. (The reason for placing two strips right sides together and then cutting them is so you end up with both right-hand and left-hand trapezoid pieces.)

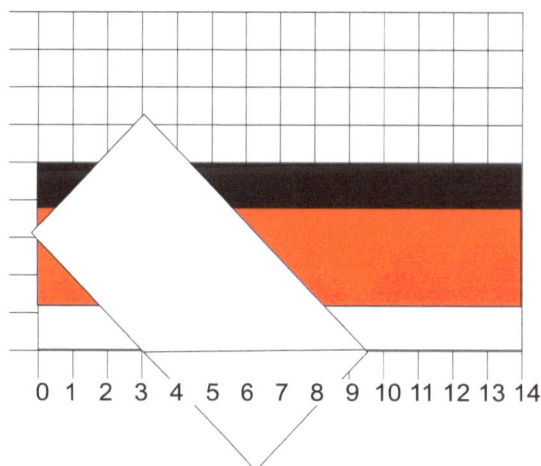

0 1 2 3 4 5 6 7 8 9 10 11 12 13 14

5. **Repeat with all strip sets.** Using the same instructions as in Step 4 cut the rest of your strip sets into braid trapezoids. Separate your braid trapezoid pieces into four piles:

one pile has the left hand pieces with the narrow lighter color strip on the bottom, one pile has the right-hand pieces with the narrow lighter color on the bottom, one pile has the left-hand pieces with the darker color strip on the bottom and the last pile has the right-hand pieces with the darker color strip on the bottom.

6. **Arrange your braid trapezoids.** In order for the pattern to appear with each wider braid piece bracketed by both lighter and darker strips, you need to sew two separate braids using the pieces you have already cut. Using the diagram below as your guide, arrange your braid pieces prior to sewing; the first six pieces are shown.

Note the placement of the braid pieces and the position of the light and dark strips: in one braid, all of the left-hand pieces have a longer lighter strip and a shorter dark strip versus the second braid where all of the left-hand pieces have a longer dark strip and a shorter light strip. The right-hand pieces are the reverse of the left-hand pieces in both braids.

7. **Start sewing a braid.** Refer to the diagram below. Take a right-hand trapezoid and place it right sides together on top of a left-hand trapezoid. Sew the seam where the two trapezoids will intersect. Then add a left-hand trapezoid on top of the left side of your braid: turn it on top of what you have sewn, right-sides together, and sew the seam where the trapezoids will intersect.

8. **Press your braid seams and continue sewing your braid.** After sewing the first two pieces in each braid, press the seams toward the bottom. Continue to sew braid pieces, pressing each seam towards the bottom (away from where you are adding additional braid pieces). Use all braid pieces. (Your braid should measure 9½" wide.)

9. **Cut four 54" braid segments.** From your two long braids, cut four 54" braid segments.

10. **Cut and sew your white sashing.** From your white fabric, cut nine 1½" by width of fabric strips. Seam them together to make one very long strip. Trim the long strip into five 54" lengths.

11. **Arrange your braid segments and sew your sashing.** Arrange your four braid strips to your liking (either each segment going in the same direction as in the pattern cover photo or reversing the braid direction in every other braid as in the piecing diagram, below). Sew a sashing strip between the four braid segments and to the left and right sides of your braid. Press the seams away from the white sashing strips. Measure the top and bottom of your quilt top and cut and sew a white 1½" sashing strip to the top and bottom of your quilt top. Press the seams away from the white sashing strips.

12. **Cut and sew your black border fabric.** From your two yards of outside border fabric, cut four 6½" length of fabric strips. Measure your quilt sides and trim two strips to the average of these lengths. Sew them to the left and right sides of your quilt top; press the seams toward the black. Measure the top and bottom of your quilt top and cut these two long black border strips to this length. Sew them to the top and bottom of your quilt top. Press the seams toward the black.

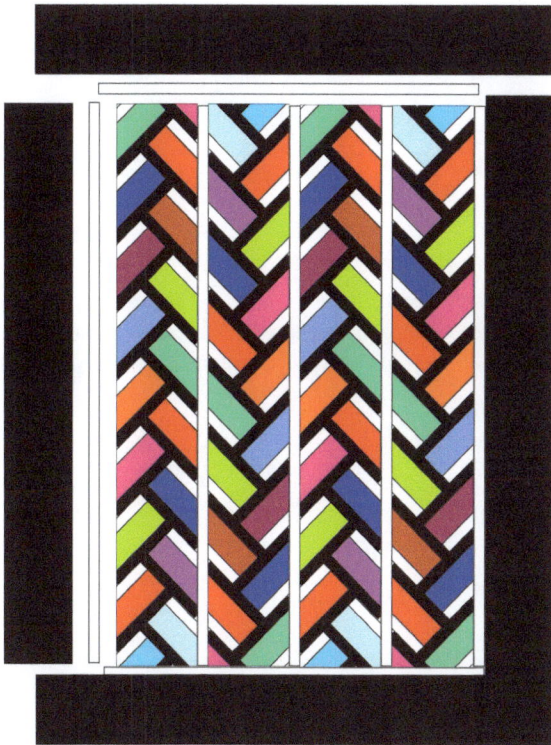

13. **Seam your backing fabric and prepare your quilt top for quilting.** Trim any loose threads, square up your quilt top, and cut and seam together your backing fabric. Make sure your quilt top is properly pressed and square.

14. **Layer your backing fabric, batting, and quilt top together and quilt it OR deliver them to your long arm quilter.**

15. **After quilting, trim the quilt so that it is square and bind it.** Use the leftover outside border fabric for your binding strips.

## Color Options

Here are two other color options:

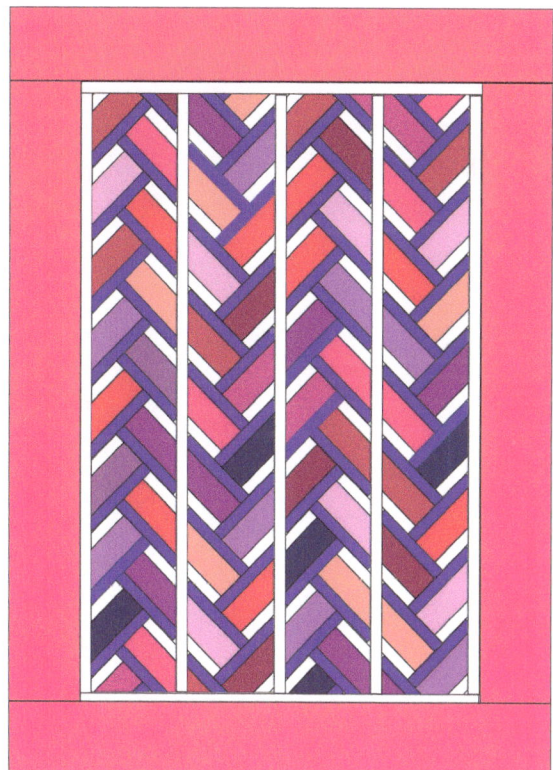

# Focus on the Dove

Finished Quilt 60½" by 78½", Finished block 9", 35 blocks, 5 blocks x 7 blocks

This quilt is designed to highlight a focus fabric. There are only two types of quilt blocks in this quilt: a framed square of your focus fabric and a braid block which is made by sewing and cutting a large braid into blocks. This is the same braid construction as in the **Big Modern Braid** quilt. This quilt is easy to scale up or down as each row and each column of blocks finishes to 9 inches.

The focus fabric in this quilt was Fay Nicoll's Dove of Peace fabric (www.FayNicollJudaicaDesigns.com or www.SunshineSewing.com). It is also available with a navy background or a white background.

# Fabric Requirements

| Focus Fabrics | • 1⅓ to 1½ yards for large focus fabric squares (the larger fabric requirement allows extra room for determining exactly where on the fabric you cut your focus fabric squares<br>• ⅔ yard for framing the squares |
|---|---|
| Border Fabrics | • Outside Border: 2 yards (used for binding too)<br>• Middle Border: ¼ yard<br>• Inner Border: ⅓ yard |
| Braid Fabrics | • ⅛ yard each of ten fabrics for wide braids OR ¼ yard of five fabrics<br>• ½ yard each of two contracting fabrics used on either side of wide braid strips |
| Binding | Included in fabric requirement for outside border |
| Backing Fabric | 5 yards (includes additional 12" in both width and length to allow for long arm quilting) |
| Batting | 72x90" (includes additional 12" in both width and length to allow for long arm quilting) |

# Construction

1. **Cut your braid strips.** From your wide braid fabrics, cut ten 3" by width of fabric strips. From each of your 2 contrasting narrow braid fabrics, cut ten 1½" width of fabric strips.

2. **Sew 10 braid fabric strips.** For each of your ten 3" by width of fabric strips, sew one light and one dark narrow braid fabric strip to each side of your 3" by width of fabric strips. Press toward the darker strips.

3. **Cut each braid strip set into three 14" pieces.** Trim off the selvedge from one end of each braid strip set and trim the strip set into three 14" long pieces. You should have forty-eight 14" long pieces.

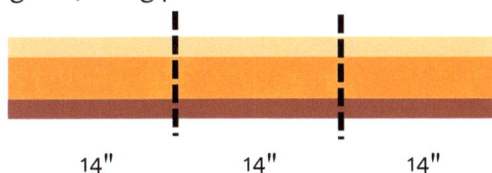

14"     14"     14"

4. **Cut your braid trapezoids.** Place two of the same 14" strips right sides together and place on your cutting mat, aligning the bottom left-hand sides with the "o" on your mat; the right-hand bottom corner should align with the 14" marking on your mat. Using your acrylic ruler, align the ruler's 45 degree line with the bottom horizontal "o" line with the bottom right-hand corner on the 9½" space on the mat (refer to the diagram below). Cut along the right-hand edge of the ruler to cut your strips into two pieces. (The reason for placing two strips right sides together and then cutting them is so you end up with both right-hand and left-hand trapezoid pieces.)

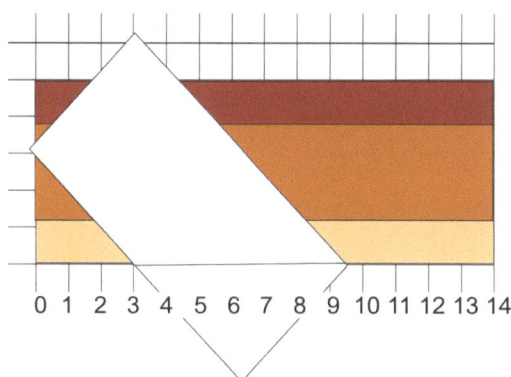

0 1 2 3 4 5 6 7 8 9 10 11 12 13 14

5. **Repeat with all strip sets.** Cut the rest of your strip sets into braid trapezoids.

Separate your braid trapezoid pieces into four piles: one pile has the left hand pieces with the narrow lighter color strip on the bottom, one pile has the right-hand pieces with the narrow lighter color on the bottom, one pile has the left-hand pieces with the darker color strip on the bottom and the last pile has the right-hand pieces with the darker color strip on the bottom.

6. **Sew your braid trapezoids into a braid.** In order for the pattern to appear with each wider braid piece bracketed by both lighter and darker strips, you need to sew two separate braids. Using the diagram below as your guide, sew two braids; the first four pieces are shown. Note the position of the darker strips in each braid, especially at the beginning of the braid.

Note the placement of the braid pieces and the position of the light and dark strips: in one braid, all of the left-hand pieces have a longer lighter strip and a shorter dark strip versus the second braid where all of the left-hand pieces have a longer dark strip and a shorter light strip. The right-hand pieces are the reverse of the left-hand pieces in both braids. This is how you sew the braid:

Line up a left and a right hand trapezoid piece (a). With right sides together, flip a right hand trapezoid onto the left side trapezoid matching the outside border (b). Sew the seam where the two pieces will meet, finger press the seam and flip open (c). Repeat the procedure with the next trapezoid piece (d).

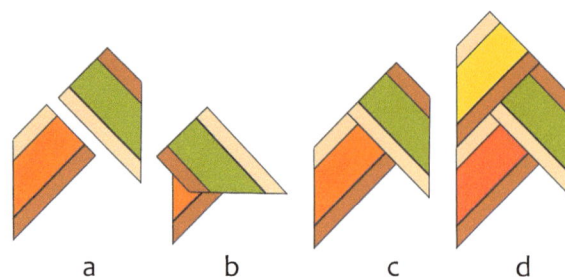

a    b    c    d

7. **Press your braid seams and continue sewing your braid.** After sewing the first two pieces in each braid, press the seams toward the bottom. Continue to sew braid pieces, pressing each seam towards the bottom (away from where you are adding additional braid pieces). Use all braid pieces. Your braid should measure 9½" wide; if it doesn't, don't worry, see the note at the end of the next step.)

8. **Cut your braid into squares.** Trim one end of your braid square with the rest of the braid and then cut your braids into 9½" squares. Adjust the braid as needed when cutting your squares to minimize tiny braid pieces at each end of your braid squares. You need seventeen braid squares. Depending on how you have sewn your braids, you should end up with one or more extra braid squares.

9 1/2"

**NOTE:** If your braid did not measure 9½" wide, cut your braid into 9" long blocks and then trim each block to 9" squares.

9. **Cut your focus fabric for your focus fabric blocks.**
*If your braid blocks are 9½" square,* you need 18 8½" focus fabric squares. Cut your focus fabric into five 8½" width of fabric strips and subcut these into four 8½" squares (two will be extra). Note that the fabric requirements allow some leeway into cutting both your strips and blocks—feel free to adjust where you cut your 8½" width of fabric strips and your four 8½" squares to ensure the most

attractive squares. If you prefer you can also "fussy cut"—pick the specific places where you your 8½" squares.

*If your braid blocks are 9" square,* you need 18 8" focus fabric squares. Cut your focus fabric into four 8" width of fabric strips and subcut these into five 8" squares (two will be extra). Note that the fabric requirements allow some leeway into cutting both your strips and blocks—feel free to adjust where you cut your 8" width of fabric strips and your five 8" squares to ensure the most attractive squares. If you prefer you can also "fussy cut"—pick the specific places where you your 8" squares.

10. **Cut your focus fabric framing strips.** From your focus fabric framing square fabric, cut 18 1" width of fabric strips.

    **If your braid blocks are 9½" square,** subcut each strip into two 8½" and two 9½" pieces.

    **If your braid blocks are 9" square,** subcut each strip into two 8" and two 9" pieces.

11. **Sew your focus fabric framing strips to your focus fabric squares; make 18 blocks.**

    *If your braid blocks are 9½" square,* for each focus fabric square, sew one 8½" focus fabric framing strip to the left-side of the focus fabric squares and sew one 8½" focus fabric framing strip to the right-side of the focus fabric squares. Press the seams away from the focus fabric square. Sew one 9½" focus fabric framing strip to the top and bottom of each focus fabric square and press the seams away from the focus fabric square.

    *If your braid blocks are 9" square,* follow the instructions above but sew 8" framing strips to left and right sides of your focus fabric blocks and sew 9" framing strips to the other two sides.

12. **Arrange your blocks.** Refer to the diagram below and arrange your focus fabric and braid blocks, five blocks across and seven blocks down. Make sure to alternate the direction of the braid blocks in every row. (Note: you can have focus fabric squares at the outside corners of your quilt as in the diagram below or have braid blocks at the corners of your quilt as in the picture at the front of this pattern. If you want braid blocks at the corners, you need eighteen braid blocks and seventeen focus fabric blocks.)

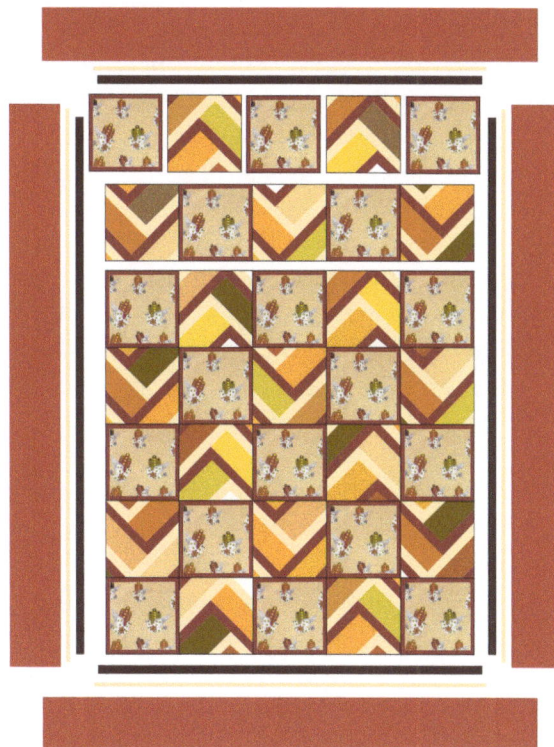

13. **Sew your framed focus fabric and braid blocks together.** Sew each row together alternating the direction when press the blocks to help ensure your quilt top is square: press the seams of the odd numbered rows to the right and the seams of the even numbered rows to the left. This also helps when sewing the rows together as you can "nest" the seams from each row together. Sew the rows together and again alternate the direction in which you press the seams.

14. **Cut and sew your inner border.** For the inner border, cut six 1½" width of fabric strips from your inner border fabric. Seam two sets of strips end to end to form two long strips. Measure the length of your quilt top on the left and right sides—they should be the same size; if not check your seams and pressing

before continuing. Cut two inner border strips from your long strips and sew to the left and right sides of your quilt top. Press the seams toward the quilt top. Take the left over pieces from your long border strips and sew one each to your width of fabric strips. Measure the width of your quilt top, trim the strips to this measurement and sew to the top and bottom of your quilt top. Press the seams toward your quilt top.

15. **Cut and sew your middle border.** For the middle border, cut six 1" width of fabric strips from your middle border fabric. Seam two sets of strips end to end to form two long strips. Measure the length of your quilt top on the left and right sides—they should be the same size; if not check your seams and pressing before continuing. Cut two middle border strips from your long strips and sew to the left and right sides of your quilt top. Press the seams toward the quilt top. Take the left over pieces from your long border strips and sew one each to your width of fabric strips. Measure the width of your quilt top, trim strips to this measurement and sew to the top and bottom of your quilt top. Press seams toward your quilt top.

16. **Cut and sew your outside border strips.** For the outside border, measure the length of

your quilt top. Trim the length of your outside border fabric to this dimension—this way you will have continuous borders without seams (and with the leftover fabric you will also have longer pieces to sew together for your binding strips). Cut four 6½" by length of fabric strips from your trimmed to length outside border fabric. Sew one strip to the left and one strip to the right of your quilt top. Press seams toward outside borders. Measure the top and bottom of your quilt top and trim the two remaining outside border strips to this measurement. Sew one strip to the top and one strip to the bottom of your quilt top. Press seams toward outside borders.

17. **Seam your backing fabric and prepare your quilt top for quilting.** Trim any loose threads, square up your quilt top, and cut and seam together your backing fabric. Make sure your quilt top is properly pressed and square.

18. **Layer your backing fabric, batting, and quilt top together and quilt it OR deliver them to your long arm quilter.**

19. **After quilting, trim the quilt so that it is square and bind it.** Use the leftover outside border fabric for your binding strips.

## Color Options

Here are two examples in different colorways. In the first version, I eliminated the focus block borders. If you choose this option, cut your focus fabric strips 9½" wide and then cut your blocks 9½" square.

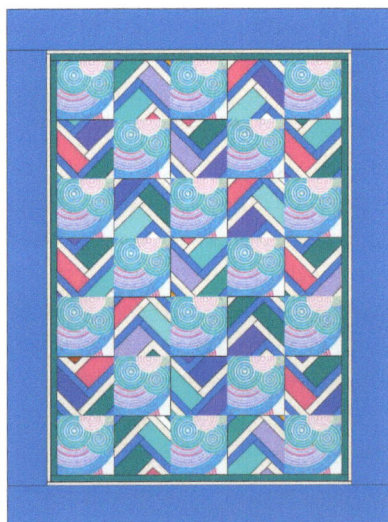

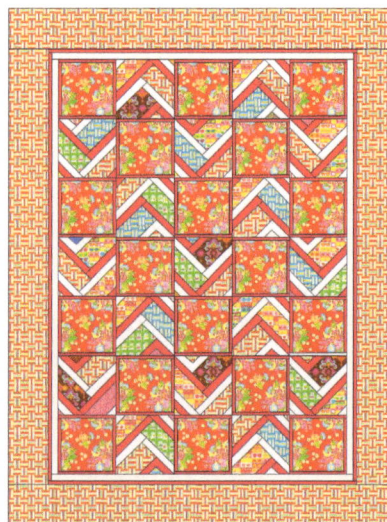

# Positive/Negative

Finished quilt 60" x 72", Finished block 10" x 12", 6 blocks x 6 blocks

This quilt takes the design of odd numbered columns and "reverses" the design in the even numbered columns, hence the title, **Positive/Negative**. This is a happy quilt made up of equal amounts of a neutral fabric and brightly colored fabrics. It is easy to make bigger or smaller as each strip set makes 4 blocks. It is also easy to completely change the appearance of the quilt by using a dark "neutral" fabric or even just two colors in the quilt. (Refer to the "Color Options" section at the end of this chapter for other color versions.)

## Fabric Requirements

| Neutral Fabric | 3 yards of one neutral fabric for blocks and binding |
|---|---|
| Accent Fabrics | 15 colors, ⅙ yard each or any combination of 15 5" width of fabric strips OR 8 colors, ⅓ yard each |
| Binding | ½ yard (included in neutral fabric requirement); you need 7 width of fabric strips |
| Backing | 4⅔ yards for vertical seam; 4 yards for horizontal seam (allows additional 12" in both width and length to allow for long arm quilting) |
| Batting | 72" x 84" (allows additional 12" in both width and length to allow for long arm quilting) |

## Construction

1. **Cut your strips.** From each of your 15 accent fabrics, cut one 3½" by width of fabric strip and one 1½" by width of fabric strip. (If using 8 ⅓ yard fabrics, cut two one 3½" by width of fabric strips and two 1½" by width of fabric strips; one strip of each will be extra.) From your neutral fabric, cut 15 3½" by width of fabric strips and 15 1½" by width of fabric strips.

2. **Sew 5 colorful strip sets.** Divide your 15 colorful 3½" by width of fabric strips into five groups. Sew five strip sets arranged with three colorful 3½" by width of fabric strips and three neutral 1½" by width of fabric strips alternating wide with narrow strips. Press seams open.

3. **Sew 5 neutral strip sets.** Divide your 15 colorful 1½" by width of fabric strips into five groups. Sew five strip sets arranged with three colorful 1½" by width of fabric strips and three neutral 3½" by width of fabric strips alternating wide with narrow strips. Press seams open.

4. **Cut your blocks.** Trim the selvedge off each strip set and cut four 10½" wide blocks.

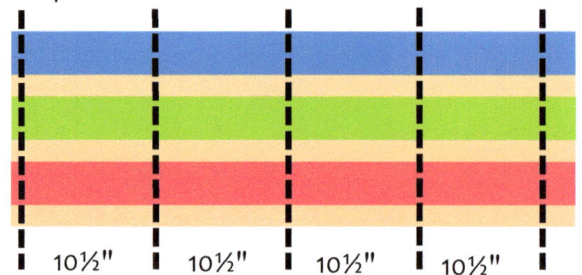

10½"    10½"    10½"    10½"

5. **Arrange your blocks into rows and columns, 6 blocks per row and 6 blocks per column.** Arrange your blocks into rows and columns, 6 blocks per row and 6 blocks per column,

alternating columns with the wide color strips with the columns with the narrow color strips. The horizontal seams should match. Refer to the diagram that follows. Note that two blocks with the wide color strips and two blocks with the narrow color strips are extra. (I put them on the back of the quilt. Leftover Quilt Blocks, page 6, for an illustration.)

6. **Sew your blocks into rows.** Label your rows and sew your blocks into rows. As you are pinning your blocks together, pin through the intersections of the stripes in the blocks; if you are pinning accurately, the pin should go through the middle of your pressed seams on both sides of the block. Alternate the direction in which you sew your blocks (it helps to keep your quilt square); in other words, if you sew block one and block two together from the bottom of the blocks to the top of the blocks, sew blocks two and three together from the top of the block to the bottom of the block. Press seams open.

7. **Sew your rows together.** Sew your rows together; press the seams open.

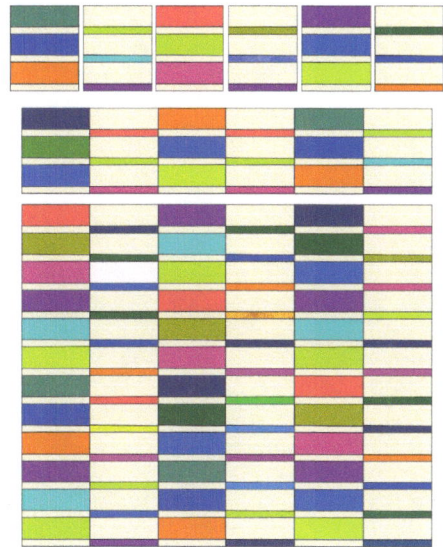

8. **Seam your backing fabric and prepare your quilt top for quilting.** Trim loose threads, square up your quilt top, and cut and seam together your backing fabric. I used the four extra blocks and extra neutral fabric to make a column and put that in the middle of the back. (Refer to "Left Over Quilt Blocks" on page 6.) Make sure your quilt top is properly pressed and square.

9. **Layer your backing fabric, batting, and quilt top together and quilt it OR deliver them to your long arm quilter.**

10. **After quilting, trim the quilt so that it is square and bind it.** The fabric requirements allow for seven 2½" strips cut from the width of the fabric.

# Color Options

Here are some color variations, below. The first color option takes the same accent colors used in the sample quilt replacing the light neutral background fabric with black. The second color option uses a more neutral palette.

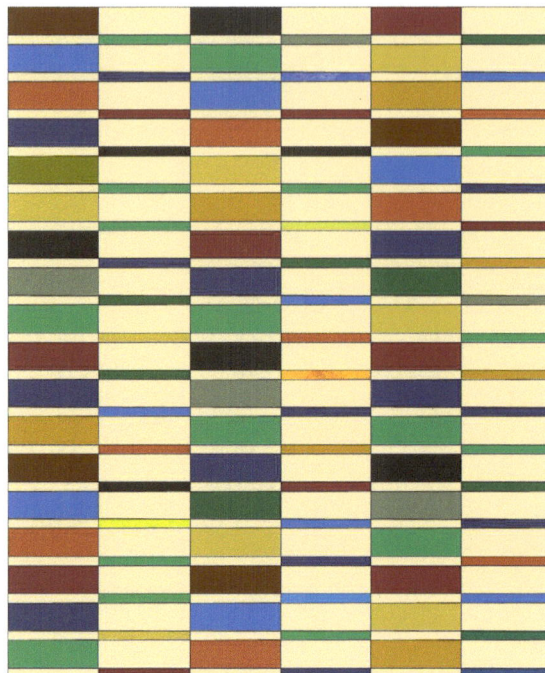

# Scrappy Lil Twister

Finished quilt 53" x 68" Finished block 3" x 3", 14 blocks x 19 blocks

This is a modern version of a pinwheel-style quilt. It requires the use of a specialty ruler, the Lil' Twister tool, invented by Country Schoolhouse Designs (available from quilt shops and a variety of online sources). Basically, you sew 5" squares together, add a border, and then use the Lil Twister ruler to cut your sewn squares into new square blocks which you then sew together to make the quilt. I had not planned to include this quilt in this book but I had so many requests for the pattern that I decided to add it to this book. One of the many reasons that my quilt was so popular was in the variety of fabrics I used—in my case I went through my "stash" and used everything that I had that was beige, brown, rust, gold, and blue. (I made a smaller version of this quilt and after it was finished, liked it so much I made this larger version—after all, I still had lots of similar fabrics in my stash... )

The nice thing about this quilt and the pattern is that any 5" square of fabric can be used so it is a great stash buster. My quilt also used leftover pieces from many of the other quilts I have made over the past few years as well as pieces cut from purchased fat quarters that I never used. When I first started quilting, I would buy small pieces of fabric that appealed to me with the idea that I would someday use those pieces. Plus I had leftover fabrics from quilt backs. Well, this quilt allowed me to use as many different fabrics as I wanted!

Please note that this pattern takes the most time of any of the quilts in this book and you have to be careful when cutting your Lil' Twister blocks—a single miss cut and you ruin not only the block you are cutting but the adjacent blocks as well. Patience is a virtue but the results are worth it. IF you are cutting your own 5" squares for this quilt... many quilters have actually cut their squares 5¼" square (instead of 5") to give them some insurance against miss cutting their Lil' Twister blocks.

## Fabric Requirements

| 5" Squares | 234 5" squares; if you use ½ yard pieces, you can get 24 squares from ½ yard so you would need 10 ½ yard fabrics or any combination of fabrics (you can also use 6 40 or 42 square charm packs) |
| --- | --- |
| Inner Border for Lil Twister Squares | ¾ yard |
| Outer Borders | Narrow border: ⅓ yard<br>Wide border: ⅞ yard if pieced, 1¾ for continuous non-pieced border |
| Binding | ½ yard (you need 7 width of fabric strips) |
| Backing | 4½ yards for vertical seams, 3⅔ for horizontal seams (allows additional 12" in both width and length to allow for long arm quilting) |
| Batting | 65" x 80" (allows additional 12" in both width and length to allow for long arm quilting) |

## Construction

1. **Cut your 5" squares.** From the fabric you purchased or from your stash/leftover fabrics, cut 234 five inch (5") squares.

2. **Arrange and sew your 5" squares.** Layout your 5" squares 13 squares wide by 18 squares down. When you are happy with your layout, sew your squares together into rows, alternating the direction in which you sew your squares together, for example, sew squares 1 and 2 together from top to bottom and then sew the next block from bottom to top—this helps keep the row straight. Press the seams in the odd numbered rows to the right and the seams in the even numbered rows to the left; this helps when you sew the

rows together as you can "nest" the seams together to help ensure accuracy.

3. **Sew your rows together.** Sew your rows together and again, alternate the direction in which you sew the rows. For example, sew rows 1 and 2 together sewing them from left to right and then sew rows 2 and 3 together from right to left. Again, alternate the direction in which you press the seams, press one seam to the top and the next seam to the bottom.

4. **Cut and sew your 3" borders.** Cut 8 inner border strips 3" by width of fabric. Seam together two strips end to end to make one long strip; press seams open. Repeat to

make four long strips. Measure your quilt top length and cut two long strips to this size. Sew one long strip to the left of your quilt and one to the right of your quilt; press the seams toward to outside border strips. Measure the top and bottom of your quilt top. Cut the two remaining long strips to this length. Sew these strips to the top and bottom of your quilt top; press the seams toward the outside border strips.

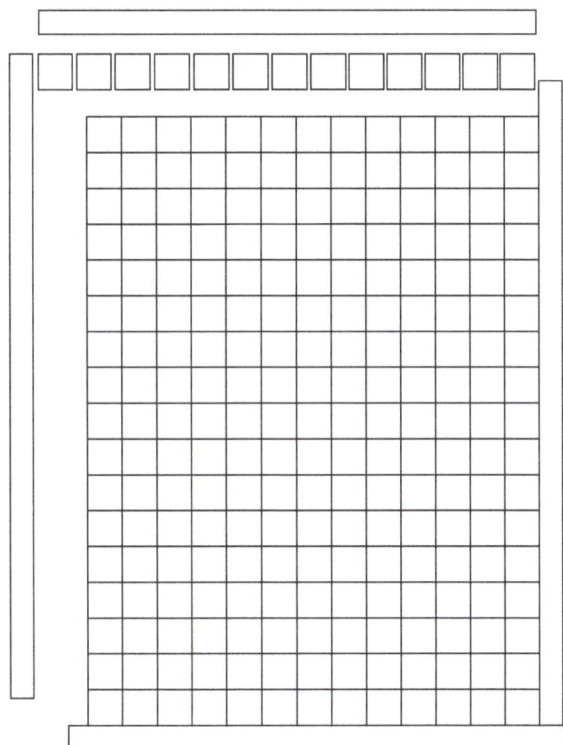

5. **Cut your Lil' Twister blocks**. Layout your quilt top on your cutting mat and place the Lil' Twister ruler on the top left-hand of your quilt, aligning the lines on the ruler with the seams of your quilt top. Carefully cut around the ruler. Move the ruler to next set of seam intersections and cut your next block. Make sure you keep the "CS Designs" logo in the same orientation when you cut each square. Repeat with all seam intersections in the row. Carefully keeping the blocks in the proper order, either sew them together or stack and label the row for sewing later. Repeat cutting your Lil' Twister blocks in every row.

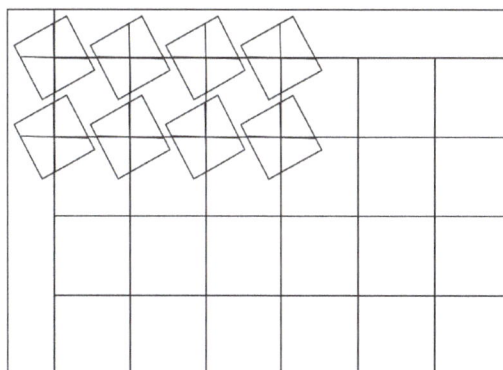

6. **Sew your Lil' Twister blocks into rows**. Sew your blocks into rows, making sure your order of the blocks is correct. (I layout the row I am going to sew and the next row to ensure that I have not somehow placed a block in the wrong place.). Press the seams in the odd-numbered rows to the right and press the seams in the even numbered rows to the left to help nest your seams together when sewing the rows together.

7. **Sew your rows together**. Sew your rows together, alternating the direction in which you sew, for example, sew rows 1 and 2 together from left to right and then sew rows 2 and 3 together from right to left. Press the seams in opposite directions from row to row to help keep your quilt top straight.

8. **Measure, cut and sew your narrow outside border**. Cut seven narrow outside border fabric strips 1½" by width of fabric. Seam two sets of strips together end to end to make two long strips. Measure the length of your quilt and cut these long strips to this length. Sew the strips to the left and right of your quilt top. Press seams toward the strips. Measure the top and bottom of your quilt top. Sew the remaining strips into one long strip and trim to make two strips the width of your quilt top. Sew them to your quilt top and press the seams toward the strips. Note: before sewing these borders, check the width of your quilt top—you might be able to use one strip for the top and a second strip for the bottom, in which case measure and sew the top and bottom strips first, then measure and sew the side strips.

9. **Measure, cut and sew your outside border**. Cut seven outside border fabric strips 5½" by

width of fabric. Seam two sets of strips together end to end to make two long strips. Measure the length of your quilt and cut these long strips to this length. Sew the strips to the left and right of your quilt top. Press the seams toward the strips. Measure the top and bottom of your quilt top. Seam the remaining strips into one long strip and trim to make two strips the width of your quilt top. Sew them to your quilt top and press the seams toward the strips.

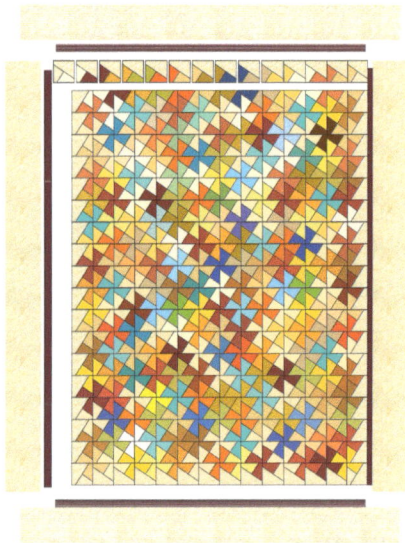

10. **Seam your backing fabric and prepare your quilt top for quilting**. Trim loose threads, square up your quilt top, and cut and seam together your backing fabric. Make sure your quilt top is properly pressed and square.

11. **Layer your backing fabric, batting, and quilt top together and quilt it OR deliver them to your long arm quilter.**

12. **After quilting, trim the quilt so that it is square and bind it**. The fabric requirements allow for seven 2½" strips cut from the width of the fabric.

## Color Options

Here are two versions of the same quilt using different background colors, below. A smaller version of this pattern makes a great baby quilt.

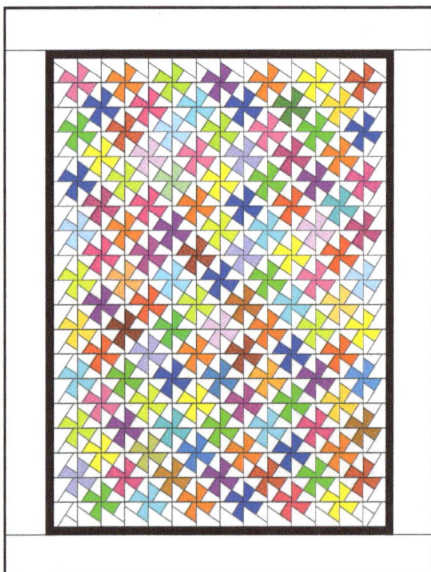

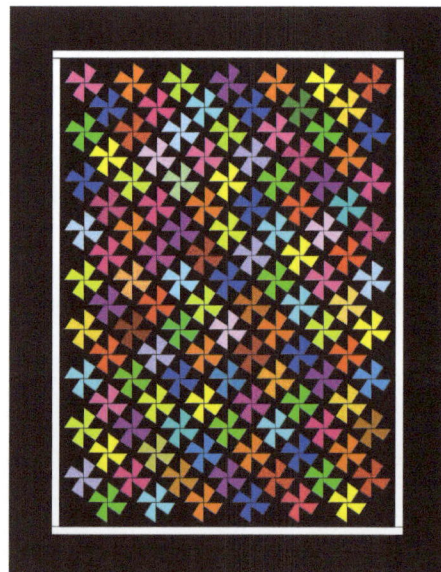

# Random Blocks

Finished quilt 63" x 72", Finished block 9" square", 6 blocks x 7

I wanted a quilt that looked as if I had just randomly placed colors. It took a while but I designed a pattern that would allow me flexibility in color placement with simple block construction. This quilt goes together fast! Using a package of charm squares (precut 5" fabric squares) or your own fabrics cut into 5" fabric squares and three different size background pieces all sewn together to make blocks, you can quickly make this quilt in just a few hours.

## Fabric Requirements

| 5" Squares | 1 package of 42 charm squares OR 42 5" squares cut from your fabric stash OR six $1/6$ yards of fabrics (you can cut eight 5" squares from a 5" width of fabric strip) |
|---|---|
| **Background Fabric** | $2^3/_8$ yards |
| **Outer Borders** | 1⅛ yards |
| **Binding** | ½ yard (you need 7 width of fabric strips) |
| **Backing** | 4½ yards for vertical seams, 3⅔ for horizontal seams (allows additional 12" in both width and length to allow for long arm quilting) |
| **Batting** | 75" x 84" (allows additional 12" in both width and length to allow for long arm quilting) |

## Construction

1. **Cut your background pieces.** From your background fabric cut five 9½" width of fabric strips. Subcut these into 40 5" by 9½" pieces. From your background fabric cut seven 5" by width of fabric strips. Subcut six of these into 42 2" by 5" pieces and 42 3½" by 5" pieces. Cut the remaining 5" by width of fabric strip into two 5" by 9½" pieces (You can save the rest of the strip for some other purpose.)

2. **Cut your focus fabric squares if not using a charm pack, otherwise skip to Step 3.** Cut 42 5" squares from your focus fabrics.

3. **Sew 42 blocks.** Sew your 42 blocks by sewing a 2" by 5" piece to one side of a 5" square and sew a 3½" by 5" piece to the opposite side of the 5" square; press the seams toward the 5" square. Sew a 5" by 9½" piece to the three piece background fabric/5" square. Press the seam toward the 5" square. Repeat with all 5" squares.

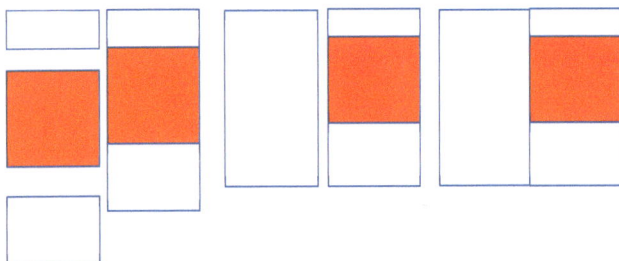

4. **Determine your layout.** Take your 42 blocks and arrange them six blocks wide by seven blocks long. Refer to the layout below for a possible layout. Have fun with this—there are a variety of layout options.

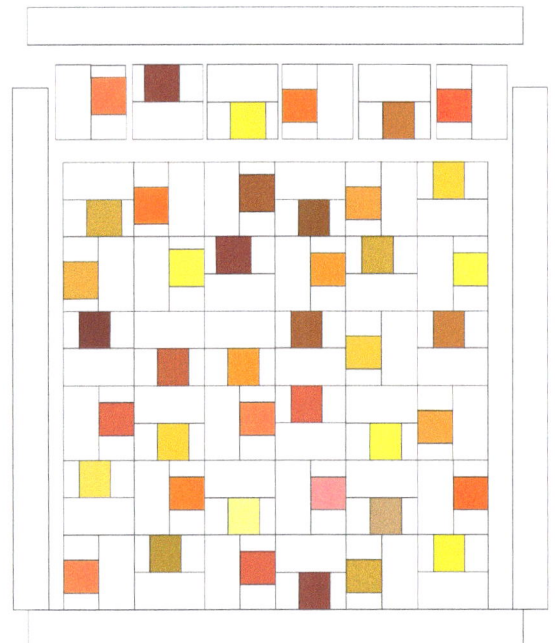

5. **Sew your rows and then sew your quilt together.** Sew the blocks into rows and then sew the rows together. For the odd numbered rows, press the seams to the right; for the even numbered rows, press the seams to the left; this way when you sew the rows together you can "nest" the seams to help ensure your seams line up. Press the seams between the rows

6. **Measure, cut and sew your outside border.** Cut eight border fabric strips 5" by width of fabric. Seam four sets of strips together end

to end to make four long strips. Measure the length of your quilt and cut two of these long strips to this length. Sew the strips to the left and right of your quilt top. Press the seams toward your quilt top. Measure the top and bottom of your quilt top. Trim the remaining two long strips to the width of your quilt top. Sew them to your quilt top and press the seams toward your quilt top.

Note: remember to backstitch at the beginning and end of your sewing these last two borders to help ensure they stay sewn when you quilt your quilt or give your quilt to be long arm quilted—the outside edge of your quilt has the most tension on it during quilting.

7. **Seam your backing fabric and prepare your quilt top for quilting**. Trim loose threads, square up your quilt top, and cut and seam together your backing fabric. Make sure your quilt top is properly pressed and square.

8. **Layer your backing fabric, batting, and quilt top together and quilt it OR deliver them to your long arm quilter.**

9. **After quilting, trim the quilt so that it is square and bind it**. The fabric requirements allow for seven 2½" strips cut from the width of the fabric.

## Color Options

Here are some other color and layout options. The first shows the same fabrics used in the quilt but a different layout of the same blocks.

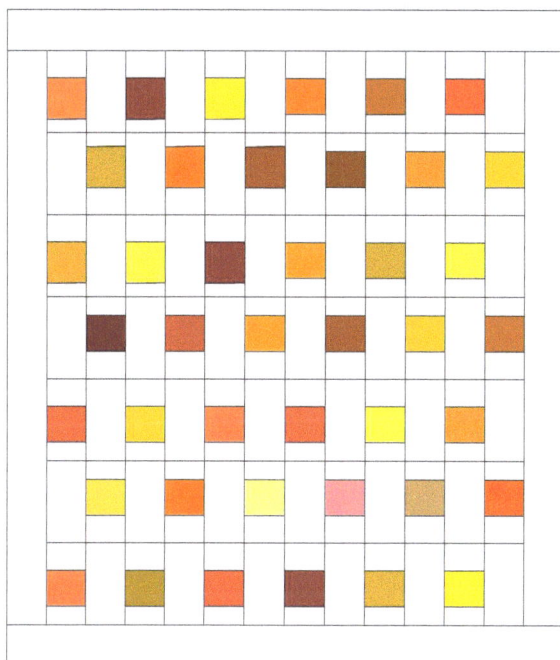

Here is the same quilt done in primary colors, one using white as the background and one using black as the background.

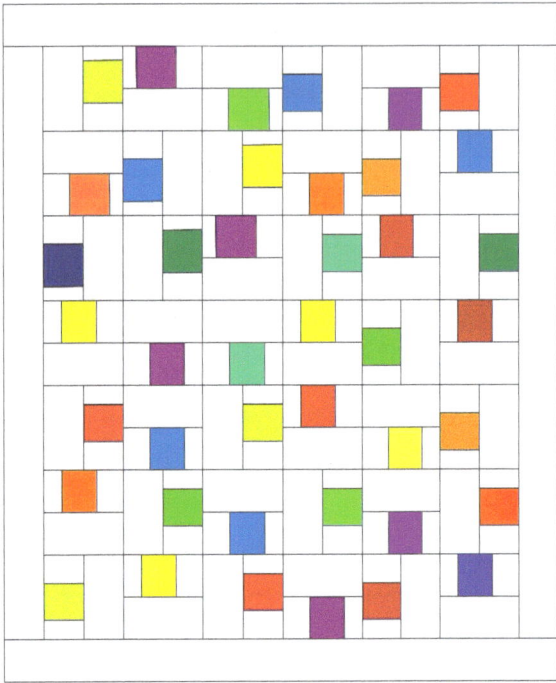
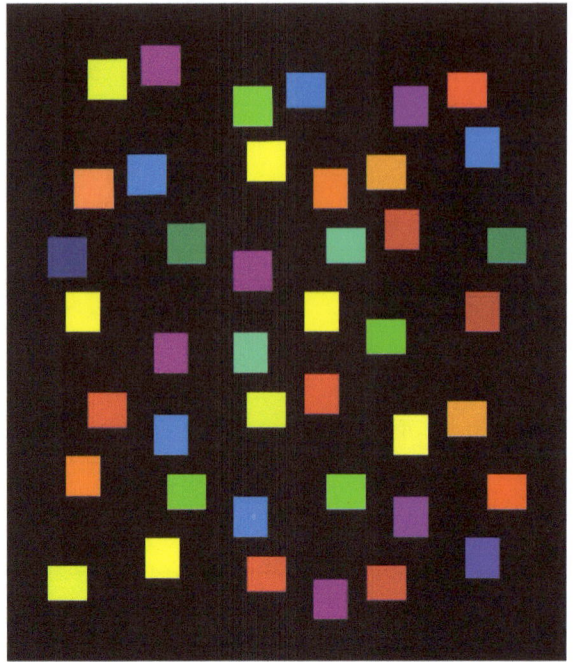

# Acknowledgements

This book could not have been written without the editorial, emotional, and technical support of Burt, the best friend and husband anyone could ever have. Thanks also go to all of the quilters who supported the idea of this second book, took my classes, and helped with ideas for the titles of some of the patterns. Thanks also go to my mother Aspasia and the rest of my family.

# About the Author

Basil Papanastassiou is a therapist and self-taught quilter. He designs and makes quilts, presents his quilts at various quilt guilds, and teaches quilting. This is his second book (and depending on how well it is received, he will be writing others). His stint working part-time at a quilt store gave him an invaluable knowledge of fabric, design, and the needs of quilters for new, innovative, and easy to sew quilt patterns (as well as giving him first crack at all the new fabric that came into the store). He is currently teaching five of the patterns in this book at that store.

One of his philosophies is "so much fabric, so little time"... as is "when you see the fabric and you love it, buy it, because in many cases when you go back for it, it's gone". He lives with his husband Burt in South Florida.

Any book corrections will be found at www.basilquilts.blog.com. You can check out his latest work and information via Facebook at https://www.facebook.com/basilquilts. You can write to him at basilquilts@gmail.com.

www.ingramcontent.com/pod-product-compliance
Lightning Source LLC
Chambersburg PA
CBHW061049090426

42740CB00002B/94

* 9 7 8 0 6 9 2 4 5 5 8 8 3 *